CONTEMPLATING
THE
CROSS

Published by W Publishing Group, a Division of Thomas Nelson, Inc., P.O. Box 141000, Nashville, Tennessee 37214.

W Publishing Group books may be purchased in bulk for educational, business, fundraising, or sales promotional use. For information, please email SpecialMarkets@ThomasNelson.com.

Scripture quotations noted NIV are from The Holy Bible, New International Version (NIV). Copyright © 1973, 1978, 1984, International Bible Society. Used by permission of Zondervan Bible Publishers.

Scripture quotations noted NASB are from the New American Standard Bible, © 1960, 1977, 1995 by the Lockman foundation.

Library of Congress Cataloging-in-Publication Data

Rhodes, Tricia McCary.
    Contemplating the cross : a 40-day pilgrimage of prayer / Tricia McCary Rhodes.
      p. cm.
Originally published: Minneapolis, MN : Bethany House, c1998.
    ISBN 0-8499-4548-8
    1. Holy week—Meditations. 2. Jesus Christ—Biography—Passion Week—Meditations. I. Title.
    BT414.R46 2004
    232.96—dc22

2004024534

Printed in the United States of America

04 05 06 07 08 PHX 9 8 7 6 5 4 3 2

CONTEMPLATING THE
CROSS

A 40-DAY PILGRIMAGE
of PRAYER

TRICIA
McCARY
RHODES

W PUBLISHING GROUP
A Division of Thomas Nelson Publishers
Since 1798
www.wpublishinggroup.com

CONTENTS

CALVARY

CRUCIFIXION

DEATH

ACKNOWLEDGMENTS

I'd like to thank . . .

My husband, Joe—
for thirty years of continual support and
unconditional love.
Steve Laube—
for believing from the start.
Derrith Lambka—
for hearing God's voice and saying "yes."
My prayer team—
for doing the real work.
Debbie Wickwire and the W team—
for bringing fresh vision to my writer's soul.

And always . . .
Jesus—
for joy unspeakable.

Visit www.soulatrest.com for tools to help you walk in greater intimacy with Jesus. You may contact Tricia at the following e-mail address: Tricia@soulatrest.com.

INTRODUCTION

There is a strange dichotomy between the cross of Christ and the cross of modern culture. We see celebrities sporting it in baubles around their necks—Christ bore it in bloody stakes through His hands and feet. We hear activists fighting with pride for the right to display it—Christ fought in meekness for the strength to bear it. Every day untold numbers clutch their crucifixes to scale the heights of heaven—Christ stretched out His arms and plumbed the depths of hell.

The danger of living in a world awash with religious minutiae is that we can be lulled into a pseudospirituality that rarely touches the transcendent. Iconic overuse, if we aren't careful, will rob us of a sense of mystery—that intangible, transforming awe. We may consider the cross with warm sentiment, but seldom be overwhelmed by the breathtaking beauty of our dying Lord.

We're meant for so much more. The glory of God that shone in the face of Christ as He hung on Calvary's tree is a multifaceted jewel—holiness and humility, mercy and wrath, justice and compassion, righteousness and forgiveness, truth and love. These, and perhaps a thousand other divine attributes we've never understood, lie hidden in the hollow of the cross.

AN ETERNAL SUMMONS

Today and every day, God the Father extends an invitation—to actors and mechanics, schoolteachers and bright-eyed children, preachers and bartenders, accountants and garbage collectors, gamblers and homemakers. It is an eternal and unchanging summons to kneel in the shadow of that cross, where He sacrificed His only Son, and make it our souls' home.

God beckons us to gaze in awe at what we see on Calvary's mount. He challenges us to bathe in the wonder of such love until we lay ourselves down weary with unworthiness, yet cleansed and renewed in the healing stream of blood shed there.

My Journey

Many years ago I embarked upon a journey of contemplation in which I prayerfully pondered a short segment of the Passion narratives each day. What I thought would take a few weeks and prepare me for the Easter season lasted more than a year and changed my life.

In quiet stillness week after week, the sufferings of Christ took root in a way I am at a loss to explain. The eyes of my battered, bloodied Redeemer inflicted my heart with a painful sore that has never completely healed. My antiseptic rendition of faith disintegrated as Jesus called for a response to what I had seen. I felt as if I had come to the cross for the very first time.

Join the Endless Chorus

Before He spoke the world into being, God was in Christ, reconciling man to Himself through the Cross. When history as we know it comes to an end, the Lamb who was slain will open the book of eternal life. Even now, heavenly hosts proclaim from the throne room of the living God: "Worthy is the Lamb who was slain."

Will you walk with Jesus along the path of His passion that you, too, might join this endless chorus? It is no easy quest to stay close through His suffering—to hear His voice, feel His wounds, experience His broken heart, and enter the darkness of His abandonment by the Father. This journey is tender yet troublesome, soothing yet unsettling.

As you bring yourself to gaze at Christ's face hanging before you, you will begin to grasp that He died—not merely for the world—but for you. And along the way you will be changed, for though Love's melody is bittersweet, its song spawns life and joy in increasing measure for those who dare to sing it.

THE BASIS OF THE STORY

The heart of this book lies in forty narrative descriptions of Jesus' final hours based on the Gospel accounts. God has given us a rich blend of perspectives in the experiences of these four men, each one intimately and personally involved with Jesus of Nazareth.

Weaving their stories together is a challenge. Some details are found in every account, some in only one. The order of events may vary from book to book; therefore, none of the Gospels stand alone as a complete chronology. Attempting to follow the format in A. T. Robertson's *Harmony of the Gospels*, I filled in dialogue and added details from historical accounts of that time period and insights based on medical analyses of death by crucifixion.

BEFORE YOU BEGIN

This book offers a simple plan for your journey to the cross, but it is only a guide. God will fill in the pages as He speaks to you personally. To that end, each day's contemplation is divided into three parts:

REFLECT: Ideas and instructions to help still your soul and prepare your heart for quiet interaction with Christ.

READ: Scripture and narratives that call you to take time, to meditate and use your own imagination as you embrace the sights, the sounds, the smells, and emotional weight of the events that took place.

RESPOND: Questions, meditations, Scriptures, and challenges that allow you to go deeper as you invite the Holy Spirit to speak and move in your heart.

I encourage you to keep a journal of your prayers and thoughts—it will prove to be a treasure. Your pilgrimage can also be greatly enhanced through sharing with others along the way. A plan for small group contemplation can be found at the end of this book.

MY PRAYER

I pray that this book will help you acquire a better understanding of what took place in Jesus' final hours. But beyond this my fervent prayer is that Paul's declaration—*"I determined to know nothing except Jesus . . . and Him crucified"*—will become the cry of your own heart. Truly, there is no higher privilege or greater joy than to live for the glory of this One who loves so powerfully and so personally. May He touch your soul and brand you with the fire of His devotion as you contemplate the cross of Christ.

Agony in the Garden

I remember the first time I saw my father weep. The scene plays itself out in my mind even now. Sitting at our small table, my dolls and I took tea while Dad remodeled the kitchen. He worked and I played, a comfortable rhythm filling the space between us.

Then, startled by a loud moan, I turned to see him swaying, shaking his head. "It doesn't fit," he cried again and again, tears streaming from eyes fixed on a sheet of freshly cut linoleum.

Other details of that day have faded, but not the helter-skelter effect it had on my ordered world. I couldn't have understood then the things that led to his emotional breakdown—all I knew was that my daddy, my protector, my strong giant of a father, had fallen apart. I was undone.

Gethsemane can affect us like that. After all, who can explain a God who breaks down as we do? How do we deal with His frenzied pleading and seeming lack of self-control? Christ's agony in the Garden assaults us, unsettles us. It's easy to rush past it.

But before we rejoice that Jesus chose the Father's will over His own pain, we need to look hard at the blood oozing from His pores. Before we wrap His anguish in reasonable explanations, we must comprehend His complete sense of isolation. Until we're willing to confront the terrible trauma of Gethsemane, the cross may never rise above sentimental symbol to become the heartbeat of our faith.

1 THE BEGINNING OF THE END

He who knows not the Christ of Calvary knows not God, and he who does not thus know, knows not anything that is worth knowing.

—R. E. March

REFLECT

Quiet your heart before God. Seek to release the worries, cares, distractions, and decisions of your day into the Holy Spirit's hands.

Read the following verses out loud as a prayer and invitation to the Lord:

Show me your ways, O LORD, teach me your paths; guide me in your truth and teach me, for you are God my Savior, and my hope is in you all day long.

—Psalm 25:4–5 NIV

Invite Jesus to open your spiritual eyes in a new way. Welcome Him as your companion and guide on this spiritual journey.

Think about the Cross for a few minutes. What images come to your mind? Does the thought of the Cross touch you deeply, or has familiarity with Christ's death produced complacency?

What would you like God to do within you through this journey? Write this out as a prayer.

READ

He came out and proceeded as was His custom to the Mount of Olives; and the disciples also followed Him.
—Luke 22:39 NASB

As was His custom . . . These are telling words about where Jesus will spend His final hours of freedom. The Mount of Olives is a familiar place. He has been here often, only a week ago descending from it on a donkey, the crowds crying hosannas and laying palm branches at His feet.

On the nights following the triumphal entry, while His followers found rest in homes preparing for Passover, Jesus most likely slept here. He didn't have to travel far, just a few hundred feet up a stone path off the Jericho road.

What consumed His thoughts in those lonely hours? Was He exhausted from long days of teaching and healing in the temple below? Did He struggle to summon enough energy to walk down each morning, knowing the demands for His touch would be endless and overwhelming? Tonight on this mountain great anguish awaits the Messiah, but has He agonized here before over the coming Crucifixion?

The full moon illuminates the way, regal cypress trees swaying in the breeze against the sable sky. Surely a quiet gloom accompanies them; Jesus talking, the men trying to keep pace, not wanting to miss a word. Once in a while He stops and faces them, expressing wistful thoughts and distant dreams.

He speaks of love—His love for the Father, His love for them, and their love for one another. Perhaps the intimacy is unsettling. It takes time to comprehend such words. But time is running out. They move on, following their beloved Rabbi.

Stopping near a gate, Jesus gazes at the starry host above. Then, lifting His hands to His Father, He prays a long, poignant prayer for these faithful few. When He is done, He searches their faces for a sign of comprehension. Seeing only questions in their eyes He cannot answer, the Son of God turns toward the entrance to the Garden of Gethsemane.

It is a beautiful place, the night air in the foothills warm, the breeze from the brook Kidron blowing gently. The Garden's huge twisted-trunk olive trees are laden with fruit. At harvest, the olives will be pressed until precious oil fills the vats. This "place of crushing" is a fitting finale for the One whose life's breath will soon be pressed from Him.

As was His custom . . . The mount is fraught with familiarity, even to Judas, the missing disciple, who within a few hours will confidently lead the army of betrayers to the Savior's side.

Jesus surveys the city for which He has known such deep compassion one last time. What does He see? Families relaxing, stomachs full and hearts warmed by Passover celebrations? Children being tucked in and candles snuffed out? Is the air peppered with the rumble of conversation or outbursts of innocent laughter among friends?

Amid all this, does Jesus behold a lost and dying world of people, ignorant of their own need, unaware of the price He will soon pay to find a place in their hearts? As He gazes into the darkness below, what grips His soul?

It is the beginning of the end. As night takes hold, the blackest days of Christ's short stint with humanity close in. Within hours, all of history will be catapulted toward that event for which there is no turning back. The beginning of the end.

RESPOND

The journey to the cross is one of introspection. It is a time for mourning over the sins we have committed that nailed Jesus there. In Scripture, ashes were often a sign of repentance. Many people begin their journey to the cross on Ash Wednesday (first day of the Lenten season) by having a cross of ashes put on their foreheads to symbolize their repentance of sin and need for a Savior (Job 42:6; Jeremiah 6:26; Matthew 11:21).

Today, reflect on your own need. Consider your personal sin and disobedience. Ask God to give you the gift of mourning before Him as you begin this journey. Know that even as you may grieve, you will receive afresh the love of Christ, who died for you.

When God has spoken or moved you in some way, write a prayer of response. This might include words of praise, confession, petition, worship, or even questions you have. Be authentic as you open your heart.

PRAYER

Lord, let me walk with You through these final hours. Let me hold Your hurt, live in Your loneliness, and experience what it cost You to go the distance. In embracing Your pain, may I comprehend the depths of Your love. In grappling with Your grief, may I grasp the wonder of Your grace. And in dying Your despicable death, may I gain my own soul. I do not ask these things lightly. I know I cannot come to the cross without being changed. Let me walk with You, Jesus—make me ready for the journey.

2 Man of Sorrows

In the cross God is revealed not as One reigning in calm disdain above all the squalors of earth, but as One Who suffers more keenly than the keenest sufferer—"a man of sorrows, and acquainted with grief."
—Oswald Chambers

REFLECT

Begin your time with words of gratitude to God. Thank Him specifically for the life and love you have gained through salvation.

Ask God to speak to your heart today. Affirm His presence during this time of meditation and prayer.

Ponder the following verse:

The word of the cross is foolishness to those who are perishing, but to us who are being saved it is the power of God.
—1 Corinthians 1:18 NASB

What does this mean to you? Ask the Holy Spirit to impart the meaning to you in a personal way. Write a prayer of thanksgiving based on what you've seen in your prayer journal.

READ

He said to them, "My soul is deeply grieved to the point of death."
—Mark 14:34 NASB

The hour is late. Stillness settles like an eerie cloud over Jerusalem. As He enters the gate in the wall around Gethsemane, Jesus motions to Peter, James, and John to come with Him. The others sit down quietly to wait—for what, they do not know—as the three follow into the recesses of the Garden.

Jesus moves slowly, perhaps stopping to lean against a gnarled tree trunk. White knuckles protrude from tightened fists and His head hangs in weariness. The men glance at one another, wondering what to do. Their Teacher has never been like this before. They saw Him cry when His friend Lazarus died; and only a week ago, as He entered Jerusalem, He sobbed out loud over the neediness there. Yet that was a strong cry—laced with sadness perhaps, but not despair.

This is different. Overwhelming sorrow consumes Him. Teeth clenched, Jesus utters: "My soul is deeply grieved to the point of death" . . . a beleaguered bellow from the depths of His being.

What must it be like to grieve to the point of death? The language here speaks of both physical pain and mental anguish. Jesus knows not only agony of soul, but feels life itself slipping away as distress distills in His veins. Perhaps He could die even now—simply close His eyes, let His heart break, and be swept through eternity's glorious gates.

Instead, He laments aloud the condition of His soul. *My soul is deeply grieved to the point of death*. Does He hope to be comforted? Wish things could be different? Is all this a surprise to the omniscient One? Didn't He know before He came that His heart would tear in two? Does the omnipotent Son of God have no power over the pain that threatens to undo Him?

As sporadic sounds waft through the air from the valley below, a deathly quiet pervades the Garden of Gethsemane. Jesus grieves. John longs to reach out but hesitates at the look of torment in his Teacher's eyes. Peter looks around, ready to do something, anything, to end this agony. Jesus' body begins to shake. The Man James once thought would be king is now pale, gaunt, and powerless.

"Man of sorrows and acquainted with grief." Strange words to describe a Deity. But He had given it all up—didn't consider equality with God something to cling to. Now what must the Messiah think? Does He long for a taste of the days when angels sang and all of creation cried out to His exalted presence? Would He shed His royal robes so readily in light of this smothering sadness? Is the love that once sent Him spinning into a woman's womb faltering, even a little?

A resounding *no* echoes through the halls of eternity. The wretchedness written on the face of Christ will play itself out to the bitter end. Anything less would leave God's children hanging in the balance, bound in the slave market of sin's great camp. This He cannot allow. In some strange way, God the Father is pleased to crush His only Son.

And so, as travelers below settle down for another night's sleep, God's eternal plan marches forward. Earth's countless inhabitants are oblivious to the waves of emotion crashing into Jesus, the Christ, threatening to drown Him with their force. *My soul is deeply grieved to the point of death.* He mourns, but life goes on.

RESPOND

Wait in the stillness of God's presence for several minutes. Have you ever lost someone or something dear to you? Lifelong plans and dreams? Friendship? Mother? Father? Child? Think back to that time, or try to imagine the kind of grief that can be described only as agony—both physical and mental.

Consider the words Jesus spoke: "My soul is deeply grieved to the point of death." Hear His voice speaking them. What might Jesus have been mourning in that moment? Ask God to give you a sense of the kind of sorrow Jesus was experiencing as He spoke those words. Wait and listen.

Read (or sing) the words to the following old hymn. Consider the face of Christ in the Garden as you do.

Hallelujah, What a Savior!
Phillip P. Bliss

"Man of Sorrows!" what a name
For the Son of God, who came,
Ruined sinners to reclaim!
Hallelujah, what a Savior!

Spend some time in worship. Speak words of adoration, thanksgiving, awe, and wonder. Sing, lift your hands, and kneel in praise for One who would grieve as Jesus did and yet go on. Write a prayer of response in your prayer journal.

PRAYER

Man of sorrows . . . You have looked sorrow in the face and wept in its wasteland. And though You grieved to the point of death, You did not die. Not then. Oh, God, in the soil of Your sadness, seeds of hope are planted for a dying world. Let me search deeply this moment of Yours. Open wide my eyes that I might glimpse Your eternal sacrifice. Take me into Your dark night, and together we will acquaint ourselves with the paradox of grief's glory.

3   ONLY THE FATHER

The passion will inevitably remain extrane-
ous to us until we go into it through the
very narrow door of the "for our sake"
because only he who acknowledges that
the passion is his fault truly knows the pas-
sion. Everything else is a digression.

—Raniero Cantalamessa

REFLECT

As you quiet your heart and subdue your thoughts, gently thank God for being with you today. Take a couple of minutes to affirm Christ's presence here.

Read the following passage aloud, making it a personal prayer:

O God, You are my God; I shall seek You earnestly; my
soul thirsts for You, my flesh yearns for You, in a dry and
weary land where there is no water. Thus I have seen You
in the sanctuary, to see Your power and Your glory.
Because Your lovingkindness is better than life, my lips
will praise You. So I will bless You as long as I live; I will
lift up my hands in Your name.

—Psalm 63:1–4 NASB

Ask the Holy Spirit to be your Teacher and comforter through this time with Christ. Consider the prophetic descriptions of Jesus from Isaiah 53, listed below. Slowly speak each of the phrases, contemplating what it may mean.

— a tender shoot
— a root out of parched ground
— no stately form or majesty that we should look upon
  Him
— nor appearance that we should be attracted to Him
— despised
— forsaken of men
— man of sorrows
— acquainted with grief
— one from whom men hide their face
— we did not esteem Him

What do you see in Christ that perhaps you haven't really comprehended before?

READ

Remain here and keep watch with Me.
                                    —Matthew 26:38 NASB

Jesus moves away from these who have been His closest companions for the past three years. Yet He hesitates, perhaps wishing He could recapture the warm camaraderie they've known. He reminisces over Peter's charging the ocean's waves in blind faith and remembers the feel of John's head against His chest as they dined a few hours ago. Recalling their naiveté and earthly take on life is like a soothing balm to the restlessness within His soul.

He searches their faces for some glimmer of hope. But there is little anyone can do now as spiritual forces in heavenly places draw their swords for battle. The fate of His final hours flashes in front of Him, and Jesus pleads: "Remain here and keep watch with Me."

Such a simple request. Has He ever asked these men to do anything for Him before? From the moment He called them from their businesses and boats, did He depend on them at all to meet His needs?

He fed the five thousand—first the disciples and then the multitude. Did anyone make sure *His* stomach was filled with the broken bread and dried fish? He calmed the wind when the night wore thin and the disciples' terror grew, but did any of them think to offer *Him* a warm blanket or bowl of broth? A few hours ago He washed their feet—did anyone wash *His*?

He blessed the children, healed the sick, raised the dead, taught the eager, and loved the masses. Was there ever a time when He asked for help? A time when He felt His frailty and leaned on those who seemed stronger for the moment? A time like this one?

Moving a stone's throw away, Christ begins to wrestle with the Father's plan to redeem humankind. His cries grow louder, but the men have fallen asleep. They hear nothing.

Remain here and keep watch with Me. He asks for so little, but they can't give it. These ones to whom Jesus gave His every waking moment for three years cannot stay awake for one hour at His request.

After a while He rises. Unable to continue the vigil, He crosses the few steps back to their side. John's eyes fly open, then drop in shame. Peter props himself up against a tree, determined not to let the Master down again. James wets his eyes with dew from the fallen leaves, longing to do the right thing. But when Jesus turns away, their heads drop again as if drugged, escaping their own hidden turmoil. He stumbles back to the rock, His loneliness more intense than ever.

It must seem an eternity that Jesus agonizes in prayer before He returns to once again seek His followers' nebulous aid. "Couldn't you even watch for an hour?" He asks.

What fills His voice? Frustration? Fear? Anger? Disappointment? Sorrow? No one tries to answer. There are no words left to speak.

In the end, there is only the Father. He hovers near His child, though the agonizing dialogue between them is the start of a severing that will tear the Godhead apart. Visions of that moment torment the Son until He wonders if He can continue.

He pleads with His friends, "Remain here and keep watch with Me," but only the Father hears.

RESPOND

Sit quietly, contemplating the darkness that surrounded the disciples that night. See Jesus a short distance from you, His heart beginning to break, His cries growing louder and louder. Imagine yourself falling asleep, oblivious to His pain. Hear Him gently calling you by name: "Could you not watch for one hour?"

Why do you think the disciples did not watch with Jesus? Why do you fail Him at times? Why were the disciples so out of touch with how terrible this time was for Christ? Are you at times out of touch with the true suffering of Christ? Why?

Ask God to give you spiritual insight into what Jesus was about to experience as He asked the disciples to watch with Him. Spend a few moments in prayer over this.

Write a prayer using some of the phrases from Isaiah (e.g., *Lord, You were a tender shoot, like new life coming forth, fragile . . . and I crushed You).*

Be quiet for a period of time, allowing this experience to settle within your heart.

PRAYER

Oh, my Lord, I long to understand the extent of Your isolation, the impact of Your lonely pain. Did You ever feel at home during Your stay on earth, or did You experience abandonment from the moment You burst upon this dark planet? I, too, have let You down a thousand times, and I cannot for one moment judge the disciples who slept while You grieved. I long to join You now, though. My heart beats as Yours breaks, and in my spirit I offer You a shoulder upon which to weep. Let me remain and keep watch with You this day.

4   IN STRUGGLE WE SEE HIM

> *Organized religion has domesticated the*
> *crucified Lord of glory, turned him into a*
> *tame theological symbol. Theological sym-*
> *bols do not sweat blood in the night.*
>
> —Brennan Manning

REFLECT

Take some time to become still in God's presence. Slow your breathing through the following exercise:

Inhale: Breathe in the peace of Christ.

Exhale: Breathe out the anxiety of the day.

Inhale: Breathe in the gentleness of Christ.

Exhale: Breathe out mental clutter and distraction.

Inhale: Breathe in freedom in Christ.

Exhale: Breathe out that which binds you.

Inhale: Breathe in the joy of Christ.

Exhale: Breathe out discouragement.

Inhale: Breathe in the love of Christ.

Exhale: Breathe out selfishness and personal agendas.

Continue doing this until you feel ready to meet God according to His plan. Offer yourself to Him for His purposes during your time of contemplation at the cross today.

READ

> *He went a little beyond them, and fell on His face and*
> *prayed, saying, "My Father, if it is possible, let this cup*
> *pass from Me; yet not as I will, but as You will."*
> —Matthew 26:39 NASB

Jesus moves beyond His disciples, falling to the ground a few feet away. Pressing His face into the soil He once breathed into being, His body shakes in violent struggle. From the pit of His soul a child cries: "*Abba*—Daddy." He writhes, groans, and pleads for another way.

My Father, if it is possible, let this cup pass from Me. A heart-wrenching plea. Is this the Son of God? Weak? Frail? Fighting to hold on? Surely the Father longs to rescue Him from this terrible plight. Can't the whole thing end right here? Perhaps, except for the words He summons the strength to add: "Yet not as I will, but as You will."

Throughout His life on earth, this is how it has been. Whether in the clamor and chaos of relentless crowds or the silence of solitary nights, Jesus has pursued the Father's will, for the Godhead celebrates a love affair unimaginable to human minds. Yes, for God so loved the world . . . but the Son so loves His Father that He fights the darkness with desire to obey.

The flesh-and-blood battle is real. It saps Jesus of strength, and twice He walks away from it, perhaps to catch His breath, or renew His determination. Each time He returns it is the same. Needy, frightened, childlike, He seeks another solution for sin-sick humanity.

The Father holds out His hand, but it clutches a bitter cup. Jesus glances into its depths. The contents would be vile, filthy, nauseating, even to those who have experienced sin personally. But to the Christ whose heart is undefiled, the stench of it rises, its dark substance bubbling up like an oozing sore.

His shaking intensifies. Perhaps He envisions Himself taking the cup, drinking its bitter dregs until the poison of sin infects His whole body. His insides heave, catching in His throat.

A faint light to His side distracts Him momentarily. Turning, He sees an angel. Is it Gabrielle, who announced His coming birth to a teenage girl just a few decades ago? The archangel Michael, sword drawn, ready for battle? Or is it an unknown seraph, sent to soothe His brow and comfort His suffering soul? Somehow Jesus finds strength in the presence of this celestial being and prays once again: "My Father, if this cannot pass away unless I drink it, Your will be done."

With these words, the full agony of it all sweeps through the Garden like a tornado, churning the body, soul, and Spirit of the Son of God until He almost passes out. Bloody sweat from bursting capillaries pours from His face, large drops staining the ground.

All the forces of heaven and hell await the outcome of Christ's struggle in this place. Demons laugh at His weakness; angels weep at what He has become. The Father stands back— unwilling to intervene. Jesus faces poverty of soul . . . and eternity hangs in the balance.

RESPOND

Contemplate the faces of Jesus we see in this experience:

- A child: scared, crying out in baby talk—*Daddy, Abba* . . .
- A fully human man: feeling the terror of the future, pleading for another way.
- An obedient Son: drawing from deep within to say, "Your will be done, Father."
- A fountainhead of love: looking into His Father's eyes, and there finding the energy to obey.

Try for a moment to imagine the cup the Father holds out. Look into it. What do you see? Observe your own sinful attitudes and actions swirling within. Think about the apathy and rebellion of the entire human race, of every generation represented in that cup. See the kinds of sinfulness you encounter daily in your world—the violence, hatred, immorality, and greed.

Then, consider the heart of Jesus as the Father held out the cup to Him. What must He have felt? Why? What was His greatest source of struggle?

What would your life hold today had Jesus dashed the cup to the ground, refusing to drink its bitter dregs? Don't rush with this question. Evaluate it deeply, pondering days and nights of an existence without redemption.

Write a prayer of thanksgiving in your journal. Thank Jesus that He loves you, and that He loved the Father enough to obey. Rest in the presence of this love.

PRAYER

Dearest Savior, I find myself wanting to run from Your struggle. I'd rather see You fighting battles on my behalf, waging war against demonic armies. Maybe I'm afraid of what I'll see if I look too closely at the cup You cried out against. Oh, God, immerse my callous heart in the dark waters of Gethsemane. Weaken me with the weight of my unworthiness, and perhaps I will glimpse my own soul in that vile and putrid cup. May I cry out in desperation as You did: "Abba . . . Father . . ."

THE ARREST

As a young man in seventeenth-century Italy, Paolo Massari experienced an angelic visitation that would alter the course of his life. Locking himself up to fast and pray for forty days afterward, he wrote of how during that time he began to comprehend that the greatest work of divine love ever known was displayed in the passion of Christ. From then on, he called himself a Passionist. Whatever he did—from caring for the diseased and dying to challenging the church hierarchy—Paolo sought (in his own words) *to make memory of the crucified*.

No one really knows who first referred to Jesus' final hours as His passion. It may have come from the Greek word *pascho*, which means "to suffer deeply" and was often used in Scripture to describe Jesus' physical suffering. Today in English the word *passion* means "unfailing devotion."

When we think of Christ's passion this way, we realize that it began long before Calvary. We see in every facet of His arrest this willingness to suffer and dauntless determination to do what He must, regardless of the cost. We hear it in His concern for His young disciples, and feel it in His anguish at the betrayer's burning kiss. We experience the ache in His gut as those He loves disappear one by one.

Paolo Massari was profoundly changed because he took the time to contemplate these things. He wrote, "The holy suffering of Jesus is a sea of sorrows, but it is also a sea of love. Ask the Lord to teach you to fish in this sea. Immerse yourself in it, and, no matter how deeply you go you will never reach the bottom."

Deep suffering . . . unfailing devotion . . . the passion of the Christ. Let us plunge headlong into this fathomless sea.

5 HUMAN . . . AND WEAK

*Only one act of pure love, unsullied by any
taint of ulterior motive has ever been performed in the history of the world, namely
the self-giving of God in Christ on the cross
of undeserving sinners. That is why, if we
are looking for a definition of love, we
should look not in a dictionary, but at
Calvary.*

—John R. Stott

REFLECT

Spend a few minutes quieting your heart before God. Think of
the word *passion*. It is synonymous with words like *ardor*, *fire*,
and *fervor*. See Jesus with an ardent, fervent, fiery commitment
to go to the cross. Worship Him.

Perhaps the most famous verse in the Bible is John 3:16:

*For God so loved the world, that He gave His only begot-
ten Son, that whoever believes in Him shall not perish,
but have eternal life.* (NASB)

Meditate on the truth of this verse, trying to grasp it as if
you have never heard the words before.

Write out a prayer of thanksgiving based on this verse.

READ

*Keep watching and praying that you may not come into
temptation; the spirit is willing, but the flesh is weak.*
—Mark 14:38 NASB

The battle in the Garden continues to weaken Jesus until it
feels as if His very breath has been knocked from Him. He
gasps. Reckoning with the feebleness of His own flesh reminds
Him of the three sleeping nearby.

Rising, Jesus studies their faces across the way. What does
He see? Frailty? Naive trust? Does He reflect on their inclina-
tion to falter when put to the test, or their weaknesses that He
has come to know so well? What concerns lay heavy on Jesus'
heart as He watches them sleep?

There is James, who hours ago sought to secure a status for
himself that will never be. And Peter, who for all his bravado
hides a little boy inside, secretly cowering in fear of failure.
Sweet John, wanting nothing more than to love and be loved.
All three sound asleep, oblivious to the horror the coming
hours hold.

Does He feel compelled to warn them, to somehow get
through to them before it is too late? *The spirit is willing, but
the flesh is weak.* Only a few minutes remain—how can they
possibly understand?

For two long nights they will face the darkness and try to
deny that their Messiah has deserted them. The questions, the
fears, the endless *whys* will tear at their budding belief systems.
Hopelessness could creep into the empty moments and anger
plant its bitter seeds. If His own battle to trust His Father is
this fierce, how will they ever survive?

Jesus' voice echoes in the dark night with uncharacteristic
harshness like a parent fearing for their child's safety. *Keep
watching and praying that you may not come into temptation;
the spirit is willing, but the flesh is weak.*

How He must long to fortify their faith, to invigorate them

with determination, to make certain they pray without ceasing through the hours to come. How hard it will be to leave them. The time together is almost gone.

Still they slumber, unaware of the intense emotion He experiences on their behalf. Turning away, He mutters almost to Himself, "Go ahead and sleep . . . get your rest. You will need it."

What can He do after all He's already done? What can He say after all that's been said? In a matter of moments, they, too, will confront head-on the grim reality that *the spirit is willing, but the flesh is weak.*

RESPOND

Meditate for a few moments on how Jesus felt, knowing what His disciples would be facing. Can you imagine the intensity of His concern? Consider His compassion for them even in the midst of His own intense personal struggle.

Galatians 5:17 says, "The flesh sets its desire against the Spirit, and the Spirit against the flesh; for these are in opposition to one another, so that you may not do the things that you please" (NASB). Based on this verse, what battles do you think the disciples will be facing in the ensuing hours?

What struggles do you face even now to follow the Spirit? Do you feel the weakness of your own flesh? Contemplate the reality that Jesus sees every battle you face, especially when your faith falters and you cannot see God's hand. Look at your own life and spiritual journey. Hear Christ saying to you, "Watch and pray." How will you answer?

Write a response commitment in your prayer journal.

PRAYER

Lord, in the midst of Your own agony, Your followers inhabited Your heart. How You loved them. How You love me. And how You must grieve at my oblivion to the danger lurking in the shadows of faith. I, too, need Your gentle admonition to watch and pray in a world that at times seems void of Your touch. In the living of life, moment by moment, day by day, and when darkness tempts me to forget all You have said and done, let me hear Your voice calling: "Watch and pray."

6   RESOLUTION

> *Without Gethsemane, there would have been no Golgotha. The blood and water that flowed from His wounds on the cross were preceded by bloody sweat that poured from His pores as He suffered the agony of a death more painful than the physical death on the cross, the death of the will.*
>
> —Michael Card

REFLECT

Be still and know that God is present both within you through His Spirit and around you. Settle yourself for a few minutes with this thought. Welcome Him in your own words.

Read and/or sing the following old hymn as a prayer, preparing your heart to contemplate the cross of Christ today:

O Love Divine, What Hast Thou Done?
Charles Wesley

*O Love divine, what hast thou done! The immortal God
  hath died for me!
The Father's co-eternal Son bore all my sins upon the tree.
Th' immortal God for me hath died: My Lord, my Love,
  is crucified!*

*Is crucified for me and you, to bring us rebels back to God.
Believe, believe the record true, ye all are bought with
  Jesus' blood.*

Pardon for all flows from His side: My Lord, my Love, is
crucified!

Behold Him, all ye that pass by, the bleeding Prince of life
and peace!
Come, sinners, see your Savior die, and say, "Was ever
grief like His?"
Come, feel with me His blood applied: my Lord, my
Love, is crucified!

READ

Get up, let us be going; behold, the one who betrays Me
is at hand!

—Matthew 26:46 NASB

Resolution. With forceful voice and rapid stride, Jesus returns
from His final time of prayer, startling the sleeping men.
Displaying a determination that eluded Him a few minutes ago,
He charges the impending doom, Gethsemane's agony behind
Him. *Get up, let us be going; behold, the one who betrays Me is*
at hand!

Exactly when did Jesus recover from His saga of tears and
bloody sweat? Did He spring to His feet at some point, or
struggle to stand, stamina spreading slowly throughout His
limbs?

The three disciples look around in confusion. For the past
week, hope and dismay have taken turns tossing them about as
they watched and listened to their Teacher. A few hours back
He shared Seder with them—a precious memory tainted only
by talk of a betrayer. But on the walk here to the mount, He
promised He'd be with them forever. Moments ago, through
groggy sleep, they thought they'd heard agonized weeping, yet
now He strides toward them.

Get up, let us be going; behold, the one who betrays Me is
at hand! This is no weak resignation to fate. What propels

Him forward with such gritty tenacity? Did something of cosmic significance occur as He cried the third time, "Your will be done"? Did the heavens shake while angels sang songs of joy? Or did the moonlit sky echo back with sovereign silence? Is it possible that Jesus finds strength in His compassion even for those gathering at the bottom of the hill, intent on His destruction?

Nothing has really changed. The plan is the same. The stage is set and props have been put into place. Even now, the lead supporting actor executes the final details of his role as betrayer. And players move into position for the drama of all centuries.

RESPOND

What do you think went through Jesus' mind as He spoke the words "Get up, let us be going; the one who betrays Me is at hand"? What emotions might He have been experiencing as He prepared for His own arrest? Spend a few minutes considering these things.

At least three times in the past, Jesus had described His final fate to uncomprehending disciples, speaking with great urgency: "He began to teach them that the Son of Man must suffer many things" (Mark 8:31 NASB).

How do you think you might have felt upon hearing these things? On one occasion, Peter was so distraught he took Jesus aside and insisted He not talk that way. Jesus rebuked Peter, then turned to the crowd and admonished them: "If anyone wishes to come after Me, he must deny himself, and take up his cross and follow Me. For whoever wishes to save his life will lose it, but whoever loses his life for My sake and the gospel's will save it" (Mark 8:34–35 NASB).

Read these words aloud. Hear Jesus speaking them to you as if you were the only one left with Him that day. What is He saying about your own life? What will it mean for you to accompany Him on the rest of this painful journey?

Respond in prayer to the challenge Jesus gives here. Write it out in your prayer journal.

PRAYER

Dearest Redeemer, even now You lead the way to Your execution. Will I follow as You take up Your cross? Your strength sobers me, and I wonder how You prepared for this moment. I look at Your determination to obey, and weak excuses die on my lips. I want to walk with You still, though I wonder how close I can stay as You move to Your death. If I turn back, remind me of this moment when You set Your face like flint to the stormy seas that awaited You.

7 BETRAYED BY A KISS

> Even so, with the meekest of gestures, has
> the war for the world been engaged. With
> a kiss. And the kiss has a tooth. And the
> snake that struck the Lord has a back of
> fire and a body of human opinion.
>
> —Walter Wangerin

REFLECT

Read the following verses slowly and thoughtfully:

> How blessed is he whose transgression is forgiven, whose sin
> is covered! How blessed is the man to whom the LORD does
> not impute iniquity, and in whose spirit there is no deceit!
> —Psalm 32:1–2 NASB

Read the verses again, placing your name in them. Reflect on what Jesus has done to forgive your transgressions and cover your own sins. Offer Him a heart of thanksgiving.

To betray someone is to be false or disloyal to him or her. Ask God to reveal your own heart over the past few days. Have you been false? Disloyal to His call on your life? Ponder your own capacity to betray Christ day by day. Confess your neediness to Him and receive His forgiveness.

READ

> Jesus said to him, "Judas, are you betraying the Son of
> Man with a kiss?"
> —Luke 22:48 NASB

Jesus watches the steady snake of torchlights weave its way up the hill in silence. As darkness restrains the dawn, a night owl hoots in the distance. The three disciples shiver, trying to shake the sleep from their minds. Plagued with troubling questions, they summon the rest of the men. Where are they going? And why does their Master keep talking of betrayal?

As they huddle together near Jesus, a crowd sharing an unlikely rapport advances up the hill. Roman soldiers with orders to arrest some rabble-rouser lead the way. Jewish high priests, dependent on "unclean" Gentiles to help them accomplish their goal, swallow their pride as they walk close behind. Temple guards bring up the rear, clubs and swords readied to meet expected resistance.

They all tread quietly—some arrogant, some angry, some irritated at having their sleep interrupted, still others simply curious. Near the front of the throng, a Jew named Judas from the distant village of Kerrioth glances furtively about, nervous energy characterizing his movement. Priests on either side urge him forward.

As they near the Garden of Gethsemane, a figure emerges from the shadows, his voice piercing the night with a calm none of the crowd can comprehend. "Whom do you seek?"

Judas recoils, trying to slip behind a Roman soldier. The others come to an abrupt stop, some stumbling over one another in surprise. The military leader pulls himself up and barks: "Jesus of Nazareth."

"I am He."

In tandem, every one of them falls backward as if felled by a single stroke of lightning. After a moment's confusion, they struggle to their feet, baffled and embarrassed.

The quiet stranger asks again, "Whom do you seek?"

This time several call out: "Jesus—Jesus of Nazareth."

"I am He. I am the One you look for—let these others go."

With these words Jesus offers His disciples an opportunity to escape and the betrayer a chance to walk away. The soldiers seem perplexed. They have come to arrest a hardened criminal, a dangerous interloper—not this commoner who stands before them. No one knows quite what to do.

No one, that is, except Judas, who now wrestles with a terrible sense of foreboding. Jesus looks into the crowd, searching for his face. Prodded by the priests, Judas finally steps out and throws his arms around his Teacher.

"Rabbi." Judas kisses Jesus slowly—first on one cheek, then the other.

Does the face of Christ burn when those lips touch His cheeks? Does He kiss Judas back, holding him close for just a second amid the crazy chaos of the night?

Judas, are you betraying the Son of Man with a kiss?

Time is suspended, the onlookers frozen in awkward stillness as they observe the painful interaction. Betrayed by a kiss. It could have been so much easier. Judas could have stood at a safe distance, pointing a finger while the soldiers rushed in. He could have called out from afar: "That's the One—there He is. He's your man."

Judas, are you betraying the Son of Man with a kiss?

No reprimand. No rebuke. Just riveting words that rock the money-keeper to his very core. The Redeemer reaches out in the face of lethal disloyalty and fixes forever His own terrible fate.

RESPOND

Try to imagine the scenes in the Garden that night—disciples waking from restless sleep, Jesus intent on revealing Himself, angry religious leaders and powerful soldiers forming a silent but deadly mob, and one man embracing betrayal as a way of life. Place yourself there.

Sense what Jesus must have felt as the crowd approached. Consider what it is like to have someone you deeply love betray you in such a way. Hear the tender voice of Jesus.

Meditate on 1 Timothy 1:15: "It is a trustworthy statement, deserving full acceptance, that Christ Jesus came into the world to save sinners, among whom I am foremost of all" (NASB). Consider that you, too, are a sinner, at a core level no different from Judas's in the moment he betrayed Christ. Offer a prayer of gratitude that Jesus receives you daily to His side, loving you unconditionally. Write a response in your prayer journal.

PRAYER

Oh, my Lord, how many wounds must You receive in Your journey to the cross? This one must leave Your heart raw. Betrayed by a kiss. I want to stand back and point my finger at Judas. And yet, how often have my lips burned Your face with disloyalty? How many times have I reached for Your touch, yet held my own heart at a distance? I long to say I will never betray You, Lord, but You know my heart. Hold me close when I do betray You . . . especially when I do, for the road away from Your side is a desperate one.

8 ALONE

My Jesus! loaded with contempt, nail my
heart to Your feet, that it may ever remain
there, to love You and never leave You again.
—Alphonsus Liguori

REFLECT

Take some time to set your heart toward God today.
Acknowledge His presence and commitment to reveal Himself
to you.

In the Old Testament, a redeemer was one who had the
resources to free a person from the tyranny of wealthy landown-
ers that owned him because of debts he couldn't pay. As sinners,
we, too, were once in bondage to the king of darkness, having no
way to deliver ourselves. Jesus is the Redeemer who purchased
our freedom with His blood, bringing us out of slavery and into
His kingdom as sons and daughters, joint heirs with Him.

In light of this amazing reality, offer a prayer from Psalm
19:14 to the Lord, meditating on what it means: "Let the words
of my mouth and the meditation of my heart be acceptable
in Your sight, O LORD, my rock and my Redeemer" (NASB).
Personalize this for today and write it in your own words.

READ

Then all the disciples left Him and fled.
—Matthew 26:56 NASB

Jesus touches Judas's face, aching sadness pulling at the corners of His mouth. "Friend, do what you came to do."

Confused, Judas steps back, and suddenly everyone moves at once. The mob closes in as religious leaders press to the front. At last they've got Him, this carpenter who mocked them again and again with answers they couldn't dispute, amid crowds clamoring for His touch. Tonight He won't find it so easy.

Time is of the essence, the cover of darkness the priests' only hope for completing their plan. The blasphemer must be tried, convicted, and sentenced to death in their courts well before His foolish followers greet the morning light.

The disciples are stunned, paralyzed with shock. "What do You want us to do?" one of them manages to ask, but Peter has already sprung into action. Tearing his sword from its sheath, he stabs at a man who has Jesus by the arm, slicing off the man's ear.

The servant of the high priest screams, grabbing at the gaping wound. Soldiers try to quell the growing chaos, barking orders that no one seems to hear. Tensions mount and fear fills the air.

Jesus kneels to pick up the severed ear. In silence He restores it to the man's head while the crowd looks on in disbelief. Jesus then turns to His disciples and admonishes them to put their swords away, searching their faces for a sign that they understand.

How many times has He warned them of this moment? What will it take for them to realize that this is the way it must be? Don't they see the choice He is making for them, for the world?

They'd like it to be so simple, a clash of force. That kind of battle He could win in an instant. He glances upward, comprehending something they can't even imagine. Moving His hands across the misty night air, He tries to explain: "Thousands upon thousands of angels would come in an instant to wage war on My behalf, if I asked. But I have a cup to drink. Can't you see that this is what the prophets foretold?"

The disciples hesitate, glancing at one another. Peter reluctantly puts his sword away as the others follow suit. None of this makes sense, but clearly this is not the time to trouble their Teacher with questions.

The priests, relieved at the respite, urge the soldiers to do their job. They grab Jesus' hands, binding them behind Him with rough twine. He does not resist.

Then all the disciples left Him and fled. One by one they disappear. Some try to hide in the massive foliage of olive trees. Others hurry down a lesser-known path to reach the safety of their families. Those who are able find themselves mixing with the crowd, unnoticed and unidentifiable as followers of Jesus of Nazareth.

He looks into the eyes of the religious leaders who have been dogging His steps all week. "Day after day I have been with you, and you could have taken Me then. This, too, the prophets said would happen—this is your hour and the power of darkness."

Incensed at His arrogance, the priests press in, demanding action. The soldiers tighten the twine until it cuts into the flesh of His wrists and shove Him forward. Jesus glances around for the last time at the Garden He has come to love so well, looking for a final familiar face.

Then all the disciples left Him and fled. Alone. Does He recall other lonely moments across the span of His short life on earth? His forty-day fast in the wilderness? Quiet mornings in prayer down the dusty paths of Jericho? Long, dark nights when sleep eluded Him and He sought solace in the company of His Father?

Solitude is nothing new to Jesus, yet this is so very different. This time, He will not return to His disciples' side to teach and heal and soothe their souls with His tender touch. This time, He goes to lay down His life. This is the end. And Jesus has never been more alone than in this moment when *all the disciples left Him and fled.*

RESPOND

Have you ever been alone, truly alone? Where there was no one to call, no place to go? Have you ever felt abandoned by those you loved? Consider what Jesus felt in that moment when they all fled. Think of all He has done and said to them. Think of all He will do in the coming hours. Muse on His pain.

It is the cross of Christ that writes His love on our hearts. Without a deep, abiding grasp of this, we will always flounder in our Christian walk. Years after Jesus' death, John wrote: "We love, because He first loved us" (1 John 4:19 NASB).

Have you really understood that we cannot love God on our own, that we cannot conjure it up? We love because He loved us first. This is the message of the Cross. Write a prayer of confession, commitment, or worship in response to the Lord.

PRAYER

Dearest Shepherd of my soul, now You walk through the valley of the shadow of death, alone . . . so very alone. Did they glance back, hoping to catch Your eye one more time? Or did they scurry away, like rats returning to the gutter of their existence? You walk a lonely road, my Lord, and I feel the pain of abandonment in my own gut. I follow You . . . truly I do. Though none go with me, still I will follow. I pray it is so.

THE TRIALS

In the year 1831, in a tiny Eastern European country called Lithuania, oppressed Christians gathered to worship on a hill in the north, planting handmade crosses in the ground where they knelt. The tradition grew, and at the end of the nineteenth century, there were 130 crosses scattered across the slope.

Years later communist officials, determined to destroy all symbols of faith, bulldozed the "Hill of the Crosses." Wooden crosses were burned, metal ones used for scrap, and those of stone covered with dirt.

The Soviet army guarded the hill, planning to flood the area so people could no longer reach it. Four times they were forced to bring in tanks, for after each demolition, the Lithuanian peasants secreted crosses to the hill and, mysteriously, more appeared than ever before. "Bulldozer Atheism," as the Lithuanians dubbed it, lasted almost twenty years.

When communism fell and Lithuania became an independent state, people flocked once again to the Hill of the Crosses. Today, more than fifty thousand crosses adorn the small mount where people from all over the world come to worship.

There is an indestructible power in the cross of Christ. Those who have encountered redeeming love cannot be restrained from kneeling before the One who hung there.

Come close now as we witness the prosecution of Jesus. See Peter, tormented by insecurity yet unable to let go, following always at a distance. Watch the beloved young John finding his way back to Jesus, determined to stay till the end. Stand in the midst of the many who demand action, and determine to find your place until you know you, too, can never leave.

9   QUESTIONED

> *In all our lingering at Calvary, perhaps we are at no time more helpless than when we attempt to survey the fullness of the Savior's love. Calvary must speak for itself. Nor is it a mute testimony. It is vibrant and vital in its expression. It speaks volumes.*
>
> —S. Franklin Logsdson

REFLECT

Engage in quiet reflection on your personal journey to the cross thus far. What has God spoken to you in the quietness of your spirit? Though it is a sad journey at times, what gifts of joy has focusing on Jesus' final days brought to you? Worship the living Lord, who gave Himself for you, as you think on these things.

Ephesians 5:2 says, "Walk in love, just as Christ also loved you and gave Himself up for us, an offering and a sacrifice to God as a fragrant aroma" (NASB). See the events of Jesus' final days as a fragrant aroma to God—a joyful offering to His Father. Write a prayer of thanksgiving in your journal.

READ

> *He was oppressed and He was afflicted, yet He did not open His mouth; like a lamb that is led to slaughter, and like a sheep that is silent before its shearers, so He did not open His mouth.*
>
> —Isaiah 53:7 NASB

The Roman centurion issues an official order to arrest Jesus of Nazareth as the soldiers slip a rope over His head. Relieved priests hasten home to gather the high court. Jesus studies the faces that surround Him. Does anyone look at Him—really look at Him? Do they notice the tenderness in His eyes or the lines of sorrow etched on His face?

Someone pulls on the rope, plunging Jesus forward. The fateful trip down Mount Olivet has begun. Only one hundred feet below, mothers, fathers, sons, and daughters sleep off their Passover meal in peace, unaware of the catastrophic events to come.

The cumbersome group reaches Jerusalem quickly, taking care to keep their prisoner obscured from predawn worshipers. Down dark and empty streets soldiers push and pull at the Christ, caring nothing for His welfare. *Like a lamb that is led to slaughter.*

After a while they reach the palatial residence of the Roman governor. From daunting towers, guards observe the procession as it stops outside the gate. The soldiers, tired from the long night, await orders to return to their barracks.

For a while it seems as if everyone has forgotten Jesus. He gazes at the incredible architecture of Castle Antonia, knowing that it was built to protect the temple He will soon be accused of plotting to destroy. Does His heart grieve for the form of religion the impressive edifice now represents? For the rules and regulations that have replaced relationship with the living God in the hearts of His chosen people?

Voices rise as leaders of the various groups argue heatedly about what should happen next. The priests demand that they turn Jesus over, assuring them that their own court is gathering even now. The soldiers step away, whispering among themselves until a ranking officer concludes that this is indeed a religious issue. Relieved, they hand the ropes to the priests and Jesus is pulled along once again. *Like a lamb that is led to slaughter.*

After a while the priests and temple guards reach two great

palaces standing side by side. They pause, unsure what to do. One palace belongs to Caiaphas, their leader, whose orders they now follow. But before that sits the home of Annas, his father-in-law.

Everyone knows that Annas is the most powerful Jew in all Judea. Though no longer the official chief priest, he continues to rule behind the scenes with an iron hand. With five sons, a grandson, and a son-in-law as high priests, his influence is far-reaching. What would their chief priest emeritus think if he saw them leading the procession past his house?

At that moment Annas appears on his bedroom balcony, beckoning them to bring the prisoner into his audience chambers. Eager to watch the old master handle the situation, the religious leaders scramble for a spot within the palace walls, thrusting Jesus to the front.

A hush fills the room as Annas enters. With beady eyes he scans the crowd, stopping at the Man he's heard so much about. He glares at Jesus, as if sizing up an opponent before a fight, while his mind races. *Can this be the One? Can this be the revolutionary who has turned our city upside down—whose angry outburst in the temple cost me a day's profits?*

The thought of his financial losses irks Annas all over again, and he relishes ideas of what he could do to Jesus. *If only I didn't have to abide by these ridiculous requirements of law. Everyone knows that trials must take place after dawn before a quorum of Sanhedrin.* Finally the old man breaks the strained silence.

"Where, then, are Your followers, Jesus of Nazareth? What has happened to the *men* that You call disciples? Huh?" Annas sneers and shakes his head.

"And what exactly do You teach? Come, enlighten me."

Jesus ponders the question and for the first time since His arrest, opens His mouth to speak: "I've never tried to hide what I teach. You know I've been in the temple and synagogues—hundreds have heard Me. Why don't you ask some of them what I have taught?"

A stinging crack fractures the uneasy tension in the room as one of the temple guards slaps Jesus: "Is that the way You answer the high priest?"

Annas, secretly enjoying the show, says nothing.

Jesus ignores the biting pain. This wound is one of many more to come, mild by comparison. He looks cautiously toward the guard. "If what I have said is wrong, then be a witness against Me. But if not, then why hit Me?"

Appalled at His audacity, the guard pulls back to strike again. This time Annas stops him, silencing the murmuring crowd. "Enough of this. Tighten His ropes and take Him to Caiaphas. I have no more use for Him."

And He who came to set prisoners free is bound once again. The Prince of Peace has become a spectacle, an evening's entertainment for the religious elite. *Like a lamb that is led to slaughter*, the Carpenter from Nazareth stumbles along, closing the curtain on one more scene in this desperate drama.

RESPOND

Consider the journey for Jesus—from Gethsemane to Jerusalem. Think of being bound—pulled by a rope around the neck like a dog. Hear the jubilant cries of those who plotted His arrest. Feel the humiliation of being shoved in front of the chief priest. As you think on these things, remember that there was never a moment when Jesus was not choosing His own path—He came for this purpose.

Read the following passage aloud, thoughtfully, personalizing it.

Then you will say on that day, "I will give thanks to You, O LORD; for although You were angry with me, Your anger is turned away, and You comfort me. Behold, God is my salvation, I will trust and not be afraid; for the LORD GOD is my strength and song, and He has become my salvation."

—Isaiah 12:1–2 NASB

Write out a prayer of affirmation based on these verses.

PRAYER

Oh, Lord, they hit You—a stinging slap echoes in my ears even now. I want to cry at the injustice of it all. I feel Your pounding heart, Your swelling cheek . . . Dearest Friend of sinners, I, too, am one jerking the rope, pulling You closer to the cross. My sins—my sins supply stinging slaps to Your precious face. Keep me close to Your heart, that I may never get past this troubling reality.

10   AT A DISTANCE

> *You and I may give one another the impression of being earnest, godly Christians, but before the cross we have to admit that we are not that sort of person at all. At Calvary the naked truth is staring down at us all the time from the cross, challenging us to drop the pose and own the truth.*
>
> —Roy Hession

REFLECT

Prepare spiritually to hear God's voice today. He speaks, saying:

> *I have loved you with an everlasting love; therefore I have drawn you with lovingkindness.*
>
> —Jeremiah 31:3 NASB

Hear these words spoken directly to your own heart by Jesus. In prayer, complete these thoughts:

— *Jesus, because Your love is everlasting . . .*
— *Jesus, because You have drawn me to Yourself . . .*
— *Jesus, because You draw me with acts of love and kindness . . .*

Offer yourself to Him as you return His love.

READ

Jesus said to him, "Truly I say to you, that this very night, before a rooster crows twice, you yourself will deny Me three times."

—Mark 14:30 NASB

During the interrogation by Annas, the crowd in the courtyard has grown. A maid is assigned to watch the gate, opening it only for those with official business. Hearing a familiar voice, she turns and sees John, one of Jesus' disciples. Because her family has done business with him for years she lets him in, wondering why he would want to be here.

Another man tries to follow, but she pushes him back. John turns and asks permission for his friend to enter with him. She shrugs, cracking the gate open. "You, too? Another follower of the Carpenter from Nazareth?" she asks as he passes.

"Of course not," Peter answers and moves to a nearby fire, trying to blend in with the others in the courtyard. John goes into the palace to check on Jesus.

It isn't easy for either of them to be here. Putting their lives in danger, they have followed the crowd from a distance down Mount Olivet and into the heart of the city, while the other disciples fled for safety. Peter's heart breaks at what they've done to his beloved Teacher. He cannot leave Him now.

Yet he has just denied even knowing Jesus. What does he think as he warms his hands? Why would this giant of a man fear the opinion of a courtyard maid? Heart pounding, Peter ponders his motives while trying to make small talk with the guards around the fire.

Suddenly one of them points right at him. "Why—you have the voice of a Galilean. You must be one of the prisoner's followers!"

Peter opens his mouth, uncertain what to say. Others join in. "Yes—you must be, or why would you be here? You're surely not one of us."

Bristling at their sarcasm, Peter rails, "I don't know what any of you are talking about." He glances around the circle to see if they believe him, but they've already changed the subject.

Trying to appear calm, Peter rises and finds a place to sit where he is hidden by shadows. Somewhere in the distance a rooster crows. Again, Peter struggles. *Why have I done this? I've never been afraid before—I've fought my way out of more brawls than I care to remember . . . so why can't I tell the truth now and face the consequences?*

The minutes stretch into an hour. Peter stares at the eastern sky. No sign of dawn—will it ever break? And where is John? Why doesn't he come and give some word of their Master?

Inside the palace walls, John watches them tighten Jesus' ropes. He sees the bleeding lip and swollen face and knows it hasn't gone well. If only he could get His attention, just to let Him know he and Peter have come. He tries to weave his way through the crowd, but the temple guards are pressing everyone back.

"Out—everyone out. We must take Him to our chief priest."

The guards move quickly, dragging Jesus in their midst. A bystander runs outside to spread the news. "He's coming—they're bringing the prisoner through the courtyard to Caiaphas." Word spreads from servant to maid, from guard to priest, from fire to fire.

Peter's hands begin to shake. He has tried to remain hidden since they recognized his Galilean accent. But the coals from the fire where he stands have burst into flame, lighting up his face.

"You—it is you! You're the one who cut off my uncle's ear when they tried to arrest the Carpenter. You *are* one of His men."

Spewing foul and angry words, Peter denies ever having been in the presence of Jesus the Christ. But no one is listening now, the commotion across the way having caught their attention. The prisoner is being jerked and shoved through the courtyard.

Suddenly Jesus stops. For a brief second silence fills the air. He looks straight into the eyes of Simon Peter, His boisterous and bold disciple. What does He see? Shame? Defeat? Hopelessness? Does He wish He could reach out to Peter, to comfort him in some way and reassure him of His love?

"Get moving," a guard yells, and the rope is pulled once again. Jesus moves on.

Peter feels as if his stomach has been turned inside out. He must get out of here. Pushing his way toward the gate, a distant screech pierces the raucous revelry of the crowd, stopping Peter in his tracks. A rooster crows for the second time.

Haunting words batter his mind, relentless words, sickening words: *Before a rooster crows twice, you yourself will deny Me three times.*

Peter turns and runs, hot tears burning his cheeks—past the castle gate, down a dark road, running, running, until he can run no more. Collapsing on the hard ground, he sheds bitter tears, remorse filling every fiber of his being.

He has failed his Teacher, his Lord, his Friend. And nothing can ever soothe the ache in his gut, except perhaps a touch from Christ Himself. But for now, that cannot be. Before this night is over, the Master will face the sentence of death. And Peter can only weep.

RESPOND

We often think of Peter as the one who betrayed Christ, but in reality, he was one of the few who stayed near Him after the arrest. What might have been his thoughts, feelings, and fears as he followed at a distance? Place yourself in the courtyard that night. See yourself being asked about your relationship to Christ. How would it feel to deny Him as Peter did? Do you at times deny Him by your life? By your words or lack of words?

Jesus was neither surprised nor discouraged at Peter's failure—He knew it would happen. In fact, after His resurrection, it seems He may have sought Peter out. Their conversation is not recorded—just the fact that it took place (see 1 Corinthians

15:3–5). Imagine those moments together. If it were you, what would you want to say? To do?

Consider your own weaknesses, failures, and sin. Christ is not surprised or discouraged. Come to Him today to receive His love and forgiveness, and to pour out your heart in love.

Write a prayer of response.

PRAYER

Oh, Lord, how often I follow You at a distance. The cost of staying by Your side is just too great. And I have denied You—maybe not with words, but in a thousand deeds of disobedience. I need to see Your eyes of love across the courtyard of my life, but too often I find myself running away, tears of regret coursing through my days. Seek me out, Lord—draw me to Your side with the lovingkindness I sorely crave.

11   Accused

You will understand that spitting scene that night when God lets you see your own heart.

—Alexander Whyte

Reflect

Prayerfully come before your Father this morning. Rest in His presence.

Consider for a moment that Jesus' death on the cross was the ultimate sacrifice. Yet, in every event leading to the Cross, He must continually let go of things that are rightfully His. Read the following verses:

Have this attitude in yourselves which was also in Christ Jesus, who, although He existed in the form of God, did not regard equality with God a thing to be grasped, but emptied Himself, taking the form of a bond-servant, and being made in the likeness of men. Being found in appearance as a man, He humbled Himself by becoming obedient to the point of death, even death on a cross.

—Philippians 2:5–8 NASB

For you know the grace of our Lord Jesus Christ, that though He was rich, yet for your sake He became poor, so that you through His poverty might become rich.

—2 Corinthians 8:9 NASB

What specific things did Jesus give up in coming to redeem you? Speak these things aloud in a prayer of thanksgiving from your heart.

READ

> *But Jesus kept silent.*
> —Matthew 26:63 NASB

By now almost the entire Sanhedrin has gathered in the palace of their chief priest. Caiaphas is confident they will convict the Carpenter from Nazareth of blasphemy. The law requires nothing short of death for such a charge. He flushes in anticipation.

Weariness is beginning to show on Jesus' face. He waits quietly while Caiaphas summons the witnesses. One by one they bring charges against Him, but no two are alike. Every priest knows that the law requires two witnesses to convict.

Caiaphas scowls, calling for more testimony. Finally one man proclaims that he heard Jesus plotting to destroy the temple. Another agrees, but the details of their stories don't match.

Frustrated at the weakness of their case, Caiaphas addresses Jesus, who has not yet spoken. "Do You not answer? What is it that these men are testifying against You?"

But Jesus kept silent. Every member of the council watches their leader to see how he will handle the prisoner's impudence. Things aren't going according to plan.

In a flash, Caiaphas sees his political power and social prestige vanishing before his eyes. Storming from his lofty chair, he thrusts a bony finger in Jesus' face. "I command You, by the living God, tell us whether You are the Christ, the Son of God."

His voice echoes throughout the chamber. Jesus raises His eyes and surprises everyone by answering: "I am. There will come a time when you will see the Son of Man sitting at the right hand of power, and coming with the clouds of heaven."

"BLASPHEMY!" Caiaphas screams as the room breaks into angry chatter.

He rips his cloak down the center seam, signaling his offense at Jesus' claims. *How dare He quote the sacred Scriptures like that? How dare He speak with such audacity! He signs His own death sentence.*

"We have all the witnesses we need right here! You have heard it for yourselves. What do you think?"

In unison they cry: "He deserves death!"

Chaos ensues as some of the council members rush up to Jesus. Gathering around Him, they begin to push Him back and forth. Hands tied and unable to catch His balance, He stumbles, completely at their mercy.

Something wet hits His neck, then His chin, His cheek, His eye, until His face is covered. What must it be like to realize people are spitting at you? To know you are the object of such utter contempt? To be incapable of even wiping the filthy spittle from your face?

One of the temple guards grabs his own sash and blindfolds Jesus.

Whack.

"Who hit You? Tell us if You know—why don't You prophesy for us?"

Whack.

Laughter fills the room. "Come on, *Messiah*. Tell us who hit You that time. Surely You know—after all, You *are* the Son of God."

Does He long to respond? To astound them with answers in the midst of their juvenile cruelty? To prove in this absurd arena His claim to Deity?

Whack.

Whack.

Whack.

Jesus staggers with each blow, but those around Him are too caught up in their game to care about His condition. Dizzy and weak, He finally gives in, letting them throw Him about.

The wounds have begun in earnest for the sacrificial Lamb. Vile and vain, the religious leaders taunt Him—jeering, spitting, and pummeling His face with their palms.

But Jesus kept silent. Not a word passes His lips, either in protest or in pain.

Finally they tire, drifting off in twos and threes to await the dawn. Caiaphas glances back at the battered prisoner. Let Him be. He won't be going anywhere in His condition.

When morning finally comes, the guards drag Jesus to His feet, pushing Him along the way to the temple for the "official" trial. This time they seek no witnesses as He stands before them. Caiaphas asks the critical question: "If You are the Christ, then tell us right now."

Carefully Jesus mouths an answer through swollen lips. "If I tell you, you won't believe Me, and if I ask you, you won't answer."

At first the elders are put off. This won't do—it isn't blasphemy. But Jesus isn't finished. "From now on, the Son of Man will be seated at the right hand of the power of God."

Frustrated with the way His words seem to go in circles, Caiaphas demands: "Well, are You the Son of God, then?"

"Yes, I am."

"Blasphemy! Let us take this impostor to our governor."

Among the worshipers in the temple courtyard, Judas shuffles anxiously about, regret eating at his insides. Upon hearing the verdict against Jesus, he bursts into the council chambers where a few priests remain. He tries to give back the money he earned for the betrayal, perhaps to assuage his guilt.

When they will have no part in his atonement, Judas hurls the coins at their feet and runs out. While the priests are still pondering this new development, a tormented Judas enters an empty field and hangs himself from a tree, branding the annals of history with his death. Guilt with no relief . . . sin without forgiveness . . . despair with no way out.

The death of Jesus, too, will soon stain the pages of perpetuity. Though He has no personal guilt to expunge or sin to atone for, He will hang from another kind of tree, spilling His precious blood for a world lost in darkness, and who knew Him not.

RESPOND

Contemplating the details of Jesus' trial is a painful preamble to His gruesome death. But it is important to do so, because His suffering did not begin on Calvary. Spend a few minutes imagining the scene at the house of Caiaphas. Jesus chose to speak only at certain times, most of the time remaining silent. This greatly angered the chief priest.

Do you demand answers from Jesus that at times He chooses not to give? How do you respond? Anger? Rejection? Discouragement? Lack of faith?

Contemplate what Jesus must have felt when the taunts began. Imagine the nauseous feeling of other men's saliva on your face when your hands are bound behind you. Think what it would be like to be one of those doing the spitting.

This is the living God, and there is no reason He should endure this kind of treatment. No reason except one: Love— divine and incomprehensible. Confess your unwillingness to accept Christ's silence at times. Pour out from your heart expressions of gratitude and adoration for your Savior, who loves with this kind of intensity. Write a few sentences of response in your prayer journal.

PRAYER

Oh, precious Redeemer. What can I say to You—You who have been spit upon and ridiculed. You whose face is now misshapen by the blows of sinners. You who bleed and fall and yet utter not a word. I cry, but my tears seem a trivial testament to the torment You endure. What can I say? Nothing. Silent sorrow is my only recourse. I pray Your heart can sense my grief.

12 THINGS HE COULD HAVE SAID

Christ is to us just what his cross is. All that Christ was in heaven or on earth was put into what he did there . . . Christ, I repeat, is to us just what his cross is. You do not understand Christ till you understand his cross.

—P. T. Forsyth

REFLECT

In quietness, listen to the sounds around you. Seek to enter a sense of rest, letting outer noises become a distant hum. Set your heart toward the living God by expressing your thankfulness that He is always here, ready to meet you.

Contemplate the greatness of God, especially in light of His commitment to redeem you.

For this reason You are great, O Lord GOD; for there is none like You, and there is no God besides You, according to all that we have heard with our ears. And what one nation on the earth is like Your people Israel, whom God went to redeem for Himself as a people and to make a name for Himself, and to do a great thing for You and awesome things for Your land, before Your people whom You have redeemed for Yourself?

—2 Samuel 7:22–23 NASB

Pray through the Scripture above, beginning with the words "O Lord God, there is none like You, who . . ."

READ

I find no guilt in Him.
—John 18:38 NASB

By now the streets are teeming with morning worshipers. Many stop to stare at the odd procession. Jewish pilgrims recognize their most powerful leaders heading the entourage. But who is the prisoner? Probably some poor beggar—clothes dirty, face looking like He barely survived a drunken brawl.

Once again Jesus is a spectacle. A few fall in line, forsaking worship to satiate their lust for the bizarre. There may even be an execution—why else would the Sanhedrin be bringing this One to Pilate?

What might Jesus see in the faces as He passes by? A mother whose tiny child He once brought to life? A teenager who sat one day on a hillside listening to Him teach? An old man who shared in the miracle meal of fishes and loaves? How do they respond when He catches their eye? Offer silent support? Turn away, embarrassed?

Outside Fortress Antonia the growing group stops once again. Refusing to enter the Gentile's residence and face defilement, Caiaphas sends for Pilate. Soon he appears at the top of the stairs near the gate.

"What are you accusing Him of?"

Irritated at Pilate's condescension, Caiaphas retorts: "If He hadn't done evil things, we wouldn't be here."

Pilate shakes his head. One more false messiah, one more fanatic claiming to be sent from God. When would these backward Jews ever stop their foolish games? "Take Him, then, and judge Him yourselves."

Turning to leave, Pilate hears words he cannot ignore: "He is a blasphemer, worthy of death, and we can't execute Him. That is why we are here."

Sighing, Pilate gestures to his soldiers to bring the accused into the palace. By now he is curious—what could this Man have done to stir them so? How powerful can He be?

"Well, is it true—are You the King of the Jews?" he asks in mild amusement.

"Did someone tell you this, or are you asking for yourself?" Jesus quietly responds.

"I'm not a Jew—Your people, Your own priests have brought You here. What in the world have You done to make them so afraid of You?"

"I do have a kingdom, but it isn't of this world. If it were, My followers would be fighting for power and control even now. If it were, I wouldn't even be here. But My kingdom is of another world."

Jesus' mystical rhetoric frustrates Pilate. He needs a simple answer to determine guilt. Why won't the Man just deny the charge and end this whole fiasco? He tries again. "Are You a king, then?"

Jesus looks off as if daydreaming. "I was born for one reason. I came into this world for one thing only—to speak the truth. Every person who recognizes truth hears what I am trying to say."

Bored, and eager to eat breakfast, Pilate rises.

"What is truth anyway?" he says, almost to himself, as he motions for them to bring Jesus back out to the palace steps.

Pilate looks down at the Jewish religious leaders who have given him nothing but trouble as a Roman governor in Judea and says, "I find no guilt in Him."

Fearing their plan is about to fall apart, various elders begin to cry out.

"This Man is trying to pervert our nation."

"He refused to give honor to Caesar."

Pilate glances over at Jesus, whose eyes are surveying the crowds that have gathered. "Why don't You defend Yourself?"

"He says He is a King!"

Once again Pilate probes at the prisoner: "Don't You hear all they are saying? Why don't You answer these charges?"

There are so many things Jesus could say in this moment. *I am King of kings and Lord of lords! I am the Alpha and the Omega. For My own pleasure I created all things. I am the first and the last—in Me, every one of you lives and moves and has your being.*

But He says nothing.

Pilate, marveling at the calmness with which the prisoner awaits His fate, proclaims again: "I find no guilt in Him."

Shouts fill the air—loud, angry accusations.

"He stirs up the people everywhere He goes."

"All through Judea He has been teaching and causing an uprising."

Seeing things spinning out of control, Pilate searches his mind for a solution to this craziness. He must have legitimate charges or Tiberius might hear of it and remove him from office. On the other hand, these Jews have caused so many problems with their fanaticism—what if they instigate a riot? How will he explain that?

"From Galilee to here, He has incited the people."

Pilate is stopped short at this claim, reveling in the simple solution before him.

"Galilee? Did you say He is from Galilee? Well, then, take Him to Herod—he is here in Jerusalem too. Let him deal with the Galilean."

It seems a stroke of genius. First, Herod will be honored and perhaps put in a good word for him in Rome. Second, maybe he will take the Galilean home and try Him there. Then all this will be a thing of the past.

Pilate turns to go, glancing briefly at the ill-placed prisoner.

Jesus, physically exhausted and weak from hunger, watches Pilate leave. The soldiers pull Him roughly back down the stairs.

What does He hear from the midst of the crowd? Chatting, laughing, people excited at the turn of events? Lonely onlookers losing hope in the Man they once thought would change their world? Religious zealots, meticulous about keeping the law, but lost at any rate?

Like a beating drum, the march moves on. Pious pilgrims prepare for their day of rest and the plan for the Lord of the Sabbath turns another prophetic page.

RESPOND

Think for a moment of all the things that Jesus could have said each time that charges were brought against Him. Consider the things He could have done—to the Sanhedrin, Pilate, the soldiers, the onlookers. Given the reality that He was fully human *and* fully God at every moment, contemplate His ongoing choices to endure all that He went through. Respond in loving words of worship and thanksgiving.

PRAYER

With accusations hurled against You, did You ever want to just stop the whole thing—to whisper truth into the depravity of lies that filled the air, my Lord? And I wonder where they were—those who might have defended You—Nicodemus, Joseph . . . and Your disciples. And where would I be if I were one of them? Give me grace to answer honestly, Lord.

13 HOPING FOR A SIGN

> *Come now my soul, and worship this man,*
> *this God. Come believer, and behold thy*
> *Savior. Come to the innermost circle of all*
> *sanctity, the circle that contains the cross*
> *of Christ, and here sit down.*
>
> —Charles Haddon Spurgeon

REFLECT

Breathe deeply as you affirm God's presence with you in this quiet time and place. Acknowledge your need for Him by confessing any sins that His Spirit brings to mind. Thank Him for the healing and forgiveness that flow through His blood at Calvary.

Meditate quietly on the following passage:

> *For you have been called for this purpose, since Christ*
> *also suffered for you, leaving you an example for you to*
> *follow in His steps, who committed no sin, nor was any*
> *deceit found in His mouth; and while being reviled, He*
> *did not revile in return; while suffering, He uttered no*
> *threats, but kept entrusting Himself to Him who judges*
> *righteously; and He Himself bore our sins in His body on*
> *the cross, so that we might die to sin and live to right-*
> *eousness; for by His wounds you were healed.*
>
> —1 Peter 2:21–24 NASB

Write a prayer of thanksgiving for the truths you see here.

READ

Herod was very glad when he saw Jesus; for he had wanted to see Him for a long time, because he had been hearing about Him and was hoping to see some sign performed by Him.

—Luke 23:8 NASB

Sounds of morning life fill the air as Roman guards march the prisoner to the palace in which Herod stays during Passover. Merchants setting up stalls stare at the procession as it passes through the already bustling marketplace. It is almost impossible to see Jesus now for the crowd that hems Him in.

It is a short walk to the palace, but Jesus hasn't slept in at least twenty-four hours. Does He tire of the jostling, the tugging and pushing that prod Him on when His feet falter? Does His head throb from the bruises of the night's beating? Or does He draw His reserve from some inner reservoir of strength, something no one has been able to destroy?

A disturbing grief occupies the heart of Christ as they approach Herod's palace. He can't help but think of His beloved cousin John, whose beheading this man ordered to appease his incestuous wife. Dread must surely stir within as Jesus anticipates His own encounter with the evil tetrarch.

At the palace, anticipation fills the air. Herod has wanted to see Jesus for a long time, having heard tales of miracles and bold teaching. Secretly, he fears John the Baptist has come back to life. Now he will be able to see for himself and do away with him for good, if necessary.

Loud laughter resonates from Herod's chamber. He and his entourage are eager to toy with the strange Galilean rumored to have raised the dead and turned water into wine.

But when the group finally arrives, the prisoner is a disappointment. Disheveled, dirty, bruised and bound, it is hard to believe He can perform miracles, much less entice whole villages to follow Him.

Herod paces a circle around Him.

"Who are You, really? And why have they brought You here?"

The crowd shuffles with nervous energy as Jesus fails to respond.

"Is it true You heal the sick? Raise the dead? Are You from God, or is all this a hoax?" Herod stops directly in front of Jesus, demanding an answer.

There is none.

With growing frustration, he tosses out a series of questions, none of which elicit a reply. Finally, convinced that this couldn't be the brash John the Baptist, Herod tires of the fiasco. He looks around the room. As if on cue, the priests and scribes begin to call out angry charges against Jesus, accusing Him once again of blasphemy and treason.

Herod's soldiers, disappointed that they've seen no miracles, shake their heads in disgust and begin to ridicule Him. "Mighty miracle man—You can't even untie Your hands!"

"You can't do miracles—You're just a washed-up prophet."

A priest shouts above the mocking soldiers: "It doesn't matter what He is—He is stirring people up against the government—He is a threat to Caesar."

Herod laughs out loud. "Him—a threat? How could He be a threat to anyone? He's harmless—pitiful, a weak excuse for a man."

One of the soldiers makes a sweeping bow before Jesus, feigning submission. The others jeer as they kneel around the would-be king.

Herod joins in, grabbing one of his royal robes and placing it on Jesus' shoulders. The sight of the bedraggled prisoner dressed as a king amuses even the high priests.

What thoughts must plague Jesus now? Surrounded by royalty, does He remember the throne He left behind when He came to a fallen earth? Does the robe He wears remind Him of the robes of white His death will secure for sinners such as these?

Is the mental cruelty being thrust upon Him now perhaps more painful than the physical injuries He sustained in last night's beating? Knowing what He knows, how can He keep taking this abuse?

Quickly becoming bored with the whole thing, Herod turns to leave. "Take Him back to *my friend, Pilate.* Tell him I find nothing worthy of death in this Man."

An unusual alliance—Pilate, the Roman procurator, and Herod, the Jewish tetrarch—enemies up to this very moment. But politics makes strange bedfellows, and another piece of the Passion puzzle fits nicely into place.

Respond

Consider Jesus enduring this kind of ridicule. How did He do it? What sustained Him? In His humanity, what do you think He experienced in those moments?

See yourself as one of the soldiers, bowing in mockery before Him. Look into His eyes and seek to comprehend His thoughts and emotions.

Reread the passage from 1 Peter at the beginning of this section. According to these verses, how did Jesus endure? Imagine Him going through this process again and again. Praise Him that He chose to do so when He could have walked away. Offer Him your personal response.

Prayer

King of kings and Lord of lords . . . they mock You. You didn't perform for them, and so they scorn Your very presence. I think I understand their evil hearts, my Lord. How often I have disdained Your presence for something more tangible, something to satisfy my senses rather than sear my soul. This is how I mock You, dearest Savior— forgive me . . . forgive my foolish squandering of Your precious grace.

The Sentencing

The letter from friends serving as missionaries across the globe left me in a somber mood. After sharing news of their family, they wrote:

> A Muslim convert, very recently baptized, was abducted by a group of leaders from the local mosque. They tried to get him to recant . . . When he didn't, they cut off his fingers. He still didn't recant, so they cut off his wrists and left him . . . He died that night. He was 23.

Images from my grandfather's *Foxe's Book of Martyrs*, whose pictures I studied as a child, came back to me. I have never been able to forget drawings of saints being burned at the stake, boiled in oil, or hanged from trees in baskets amid wasps' nests.

The writer of Hebrews tells us that Jesus had to be made like His brethren in all things. What does this mean? Is it possible that through the wounds of His passion, Christ was made like millions of martyrs who would follow in His steps? When thorns gouged His brow, were their faces embedded on His mind? When whips carved grisly trenches upon His back, were their cries ripping at His heart?

As we come to some of the worst of Christ's sufferings, let us remember that there is purpose in every wound. Many persecuted saints find strength in knowing Jesus is intimately acquainted with such pain. As we watch Christ in the throes of affliction, let each blow remind us all that we are redeemed, not by a distant and aloof God, but by our precious Lord, who was *made like His brethren in all things.*

14 ABSOLVED

> *The very existence of the cross, and of the*
> *crucified Christ, forces us to make a crucial*
> *decision: Will we look for God somewhere*
> *else, or will we make the cross, and the*
> *crucified Christ, the basis of our thought*
> *about God?*
>
> —Alistair E. McGrath

REFLECT

The psalmist poses the question:

> *I will lift up my eyes to the mountains; from where shall*
> *my help come?*
>
> —Psalm 121:1 NASB

Then he answers:

> *My help comes from the* LORD, *who made heaven and*
> *earth.* (v. 2)

Quietly consider this reality. Allow your mind to reflect on the truth that the Maker of heaven and earth is personally concerned with the details of your life, ready to send help whenever you call upon Him.

Seek to focus solely on God, who meets you here, asking Him to remove mental distractions. Ask Him to write His word for you from the cross on your heart this day.

READ

They cried out all together, saying, "Away with this man,
and release for us Barabbas!"

—Luke 23:18 NASB

Back at the Praetorium, they push Jesus up some steps to a
platform where the growing crowd can easily see Him. The
strange scene of the battered prisoner now decked in a royal
robe sets tongues wagging. Summoning the high priests and
other leaders to the front, Pilate holds up his right hand to
silence the crowd.

"You brought this Man to me at dawn, accusing Him of
inciting people against the government. I have listened to all
you say, I have questioned the prisoner myself, and I find Him
innocent of these charges. Herod agrees and has sent Him back
to me. Therefore, I will have Him scourged and released."

Confident that this compromise will appease the priests, Pilate
turns to leave, but the cries of some well-known freedom fighters
stop him. One of his attendants leans over to explain that the men
showed up a while ago, requesting he release their leader,
Barabbas, following the custom of the Roman government to
release a Jewish prisoner every Passover as a sign of peace.

To Pilate, it seems the gods have smiled upon him. Of
course—this is what he can do with the innocent Galilean—let
Him go and be done with it. Surely, given the choice, any God-
fearing Jew would prefer Jesus' release to that of the murderer
Barabbas.

Ignoring the defiant revolutionaries, Pilate calls out to the
high priests: "What if I give you the King of the Jews? Would
you like me to release Him?"

Any answer they might give is drowned out by the cries of
Barabbas's friends for his emancipation. Tempers flare as the
morning sun beats down its relentless heat. As Pilate observes
the growing unease, a breathless messenger runs up the steps
and hands him a sealed envelope.

Inside is a hastily scribbled note from his wife. *Have nothing to do with the Carpenter from Nazareth. Last night I had a terrible dream about Him, and I have already suffered much today because of it.*

Pilate glances up to see the crowd scrutinizing his every move. The priests and other religious leaders have dispersed among them, quietly championing their cause, purposefully stirring up the people.

Wanting to be done with it all, Pilate thunders, "Tell me now—which of the two men shall I release to you?"

A thunderous roar rises up in response: "Away with this Man, and release for us Barabbas!"

Pilate stares at Jesus, who watches silently. Sadness has settled on His bruised face, His weary body slightly bent, a pitiful sight.

What does Jesus see in the agitated mob? What must He feel as He watches the freedom fighters demand their leader's release? Their loyalty is fierce and fearless. Where are the men who promised they'd never leave *Him*, never deny *Him*, follow *Him* to death if need be? These renegades battle brazenly for political liberation—who will carry on *His* revolution to liberate the souls of men?

Pilate ponders how to handle this One who has created such a furor. The crowd is getting out of hand—how easily this mess could ruin his reputation in Rome. What in the world should he do?

"Take Him and scourge Him," he barks at the soldiers, buying time while the crowd looks on.

They drag Jesus away, every eye watching, wondering if the weakened prisoner can possibly survive the horrific flogging to come. Pilate follows along, weary with the whole thing.

Can it still be morning? The day seems unbearably long to priests and procurators, but for the Man of sorrows, it has only begun.

Respond

Consider the moment when crowds called for the release of Barabbas. Besides murder and robbery, he was guilty of the same things Jesus had been accused of—seeking political power and creating an insurgency against the government. In the end, Barabbas will be set free.

See yourself as Barabbas, sitting in a dark cave awaiting your sentence of death. Feel your own guilt. Experience the shame of failure, the fear of eternity in darkness. Then consider how it would be to have someone open the gate, loosen your chains, and release you, no questions asked.

Barabbas was set free when Jesus should have been. Through Jesus' death, you are given eternal freedom. Reflect on the reality of this. Feel the joy of it. Thank God; pour out your gratefulness to Him. Write the following in your own words as a prayer of thanksgiving:

Wretched man that I am! Who will set me free from the body of this death? Thanks be to God through Jesus Christ our Lord!

—Romans 7:24–25 NASB

PRAYER

I am that prisoner, Lord, who deserves to die. I have committed crime after crime against the living God, and I have no one to demand my release. No one except You. How can I ever comprehend that at this very moment You stand before the Father doing just that? Praying for me? How will I ever grasp the mystery that You went to Your death, innocent of every charge, while I am free today? To me, these things are incomprehensible and inexplicable.

15   SCOURGED

> *Of all the pains that lead to salvation this is the most pain, to see thy Love suffer. How might any pain be more to me than to see Him that is all my life, all my bliss, and all my joy suffer?*
>
> —Julian of Norwich

REFLECT

Today we will look at the scourging of Jesus. This may be difficult, painful, and even sickening. Spend enough time in God's presence to prepare your heart. Read aloud or sing the words to the following old hymn:

There Is a Fountain, Filled with Blood
William Cowper

*There is a fountain filled with blood, drawn from
    Emmanuel's veins;
And sinners plunged beneath that flood, lose all their
    guilty stains.
Lose all their guilty stains, lose all their guilty stains.
And sinners plunged beneath that flood, lose all their
    guilty stains.*

*E'er since, by faith, I saw the stream Thy flowing wounds
    supply,
Redeeming love has been my theme, and shall be till I die.*

And shall be till I die, and shall be till I die;
Redeeming love has been my theme, and shall be till I die.

Zechariah prophesied of this fountain long before Christ came to shed His blood: "In that day a fountain will be opened for the house of David and for the inhabitants of Jerusalem, for sin and for impurity" (Zechariah 13:1 NASB). Spend some time in silent gratitude for the cleansing streams provided for your own sin and impurity.

Paul wrote of his desire to know the fellowship of Christ's sufferings (see Philippians 3:10). The word *fellowship* refers to something like a sense of partnership. Offer yourself to walk in communion through these sufferings of the Lord, asking Him to reveal Himself to you in a fresh way today.

READ

The chastening for our well-being fell upon Him, and by
His scourging we are healed.

—Isaiah 53:5 NASB

Inside the palace courtyard soldiers prepare for the scourging, paying little attention to their subject. With businesslike precision, one rips the robe from Jesus' shoulders and another removes the rest of His clothes. Grim-faced, He offers no resistance.

Exposed, vulnerable, defenseless in every way. Does Christ commune in Spirit with His Father as the morning air assaults His naked body? Is this part of the cup He cried out against in the Garden only hours ago?

They shove Him roughly across the yard to a column stained with layers of dried blood. Pushing Him to His knees, they lift His arms above His head, securing them to the post. A soldier stands to His right and another to His left, awaiting the order to begin. Does Jesus see frail sinners in need of a Savior behind their hardened eyes?

Each holds a vicious-looking whip several feet long. Halfway down it is split into numerous leather strips to which pieces of sheep bone are attached. Two lead balls hang at the end of every strip.

Jesus knows a brief moment of cool relief as He rests His cheek against the column. All too quickly a voice shouts, "Begin!" and everyone moves into place.

The soldier on the right, well trained and competent from years of experience with the flagellum, strikes the first blow. A crack resounds throughout the courtyard, spilling over into the silent wake of those who wait outside.

At first the bones make tiny cuts on Jesus' back, the iron balls raising red welts that quickly turn to crimson bruises. With each blow, Jesus' body recoils. Before He can even catch His breath, another strike is administered.

Crack.

Silence.

Crack.

Silence.

And on and on it goes until the first soldier tires. The second steps in quickly, not missing a beat. By now the small cuts are bleeding profusely, and a few of the large bruises are breaking open.

Jesus' strength fails, the loss of blood making Him light-headed and dizzy. He winces now only slightly with each lash of the whip.

Crack.

Silence.

Crack.

Silence.

Blood is beginning to gush from several of the gaping wounds. Soldiers turn away, feigning busyness to avoid the horrid sight. Tiny ribbons of flesh are all that remain on Jesus' back.

The officer is just doing a job—one he's done a thousand times before. But does he have any idea upon whom he inflicts such hideous blows?

Crack.
Silence.
Crack.
Silence.
Crack.

The two soldiers continue to take turns, oblivious to the prisoner's condition until Pilate returns and calls a halt to the bloody operation. Jesus has not moved for several minutes now. If He dies here, they will all face grave reprimands and the loss of their esteemed positions in the royal army.

Hurrying now to untie Him, the soldiers try to lift the nearly unconscious prisoner to His feet, flanking Him on either side. Jesus manages to open His eyes briefly, and He somehow finds the fortitude to stand. Searing pain slices through Him as they drape His clothes back on His battered body.

Then He is led out to the platform. Many in the crowd turn away—the disfigured Carpenter being too abhorrent to look at. Others less humane await in anticipation the grand finale of their morning merrymaking. The soldiers secure Jesus' feet and gingerly step away. Somehow He manages not to collapse. Pilate, frustrated and fearful because of his wife's dream, looks at the beaten-down would-be king.

Rancor resonates in his curt challenge to the crowd: "Behold the Man!"

And demons delight. The Father hangs His head and weeps, for though He could heal the mass of bleeding tissue with a word, He won't. The words of the prophet Isaiah play a haunting melody through the halls of heaven. Today the Son of God is bruised for the iniquities of a dying world, and by His stripes, humanity can finally be healed.

RESPOND

Take a minute to contemplate the moments of scourging Christ endured. As you form this picture in your mind, read the following passage:

Surely our griefs He Himself bore, and our sorrows He carried; yet we ourselves esteemed Him stricken, smitten of God, and afflicted. But He was pierced through for our transgressions, He was crushed for our iniquities; the chastening for our well-being fell upon Him, and by His scourging we are healed. All of us like sheep have gone astray, each of us has turned to his own way; but the LORD has caused the iniquity of us all to fall on Him.
—Isaiah 53:4–6 NASB

In every bruise that each ball of lead inflicted, see the gravity of sin. With each bloody cut the leather and bone made, understand the healing that is secured. Write this passage out in your own words as a prayer of worship.

Receive from the Lord, rejoicing (perhaps in a bittersweet way) that Jesus endured what He did.

PRAYER

Must I go on, Lord Jesus? I can barely stand to see myself through the gaping wounds on Your back. My stomach churns and I want to walk away. The journey to the cross is fraught with a thousand deaths, and I'm not sure if I am prepared to embrace each one. To know the fellowship of Your sufferings is not so simple. Sustain me in my quest, dearest Savior, and I will seek to share Your sorrow.

16   FINAL QUESTIONING

> *Where have your love, your mercy, your compassion shone out more luminously than in your wounds, sweet gentle Lord of mercy? More mercy than this no one has than that he lay down his life for those who are doomed to death.*
>
> —Bernard of Clairvaux

REFLECT

Has the cross become a place of familiar consolation to you yet? Are you beginning to feel a drawing in your soul to reflect often on the mysteries at Calvary? Take a few minutes as you quiet your heart to consider what Jesus' sufferings mean to you after reflecting on them through the past days or weeks.

John wrote:

> *We have come to know and have believed the love which God has for us. God is love.*
>
> —1 John 4:16 NASB

Are you beginning to know God's love in a deeper way through this journey? Are you coming to a place of truly believing it?

Ponder these things and ask God to do an even deeper work as we draw nearer to Christ's death.

READ

> *But they shouted all the more, "Crucify Him!"*
> —Mark 15:14 NASB

The mangled-looking Man barely stands, a sobering symbol of Rome's power to destroy. Pilate, wanting to leave it all behind and confident the brutal beating will satisfy the crowd's call for justice, asks once again: "Then what shall I do with Jesus who is called the Christ?"

Before the words are out of his mouth, a loud cry ensues: "Crucify Him! You crucify Him!"

"Me? But I believe He's innocent. Tell me—what evil has He done? Take Him yourselves and crucify Him—I find no guilt in Him."

Pilate knows his offer is an empty one, for the power to execute lies with him alone. Try as he might, he cannot extricate himself from this Man's future.

Jesus struggles to keep His balance. He has lost so much blood, His head at times seems to float above Him. Standing here, He is the only One who really knows the details of how this drama will end. Does He wish He could just speak and be on His way to Golgotha? If this entire mob suddenly stopped to listen to *Him*, what would He say?

A high priest makes his voice heard above the crowd: "He says He is the Son of God, and by our laws, for this He must die."

Superstitious fear grips Pilate upon hearing these words. Son of God? He hasn't heard this charge before. Is this why his wife warned him to steer clear of this Man? Does He have mystical powers? Looking at the broken body beside him, it seems nothing could be farther from the truth.

Turning quickly, Pilate motions for them to bring Jesus back into the palace. He must get to the bottom of this.

"Where do You come from?" Knowing the answer already, Pilate gives Jesus a chance to deny the charges of a claim to Deity.

Jesus looks at him but says nothing.

"Why won't You talk to me?" Pilate pleads, baffled again by His lack of self-defense. It is unheard of—truly the Man must be crazy.

"Don't You understand that I have the power here, that with a word I can release You *or* crucify You?"

Staring off as if in a trance, Jesus smiles slightly. Is He moving through the caverns of His memory to a time before the foundation of the world? Does He envision the moment before His incarnation when He stepped down from heaven to redeem humankind? Does He recall His agony of a few hours past when He made the choice to drink this very cup? What thoughts drive Him to finally respond to Pilate?

"You have no power over Me, except that which is given to you from above. The one who turned me over to you has the greater sin here."

Pilate bristles at the affront to his authority, but senses a strange relief. He has done all he can do. He looks once more into the eyes of the Christ, frustrated at his failure to figure this odd fellow out. Shaking his head, he walks back onto the platform, leaving the prisoner behind with the guards.

Distant cries for execution tick like a time bomb in Jesus' ears. But perhaps He garners a measure of strength in the words of truth He has just spoken. For though He feels His wounds with every excruciating move of His body, no one can take His life from Him—He alone has the power to lay it down.

Faces flash across His mind—fishermen, priests, prostitutes, mothers, children, tax collectors, doctors, friends, and enemies. In every countenance He sees a desperate need for a Redeemer. For these He came . . . for these He presses on.

RESPOND

Consider the weariness Jesus must have felt as He was constantly passed from one person to another. He allowed Himself to be completely at their mercy. Physically He must have been in torment. Take a few minutes to contemplate the physical and emotional state of Jesus at this time.

On many previous occasions, Jesus could have been arrested or killed, but He escaped (see John 8:59; 10:39). Reflect on the reality that every part of this story is preordained by the Father and chosen by the Son.

Earlier Jesus had prayed: "Father, the hour has come; glorify Your Son, that the Son may glorify You, even as You gave Him authority over all flesh, that to all whom You have given Him, He may give eternal life" (John 17:1–2 NASB).

To glorify means to confer honor, to praise, to magnify. Jesus seems to be saying that the Cross is an honor to Him and that through His death, the Father will glorify Him. Ponder this in light of His suffering. Consider this in light of His desire in verse 2—to give you eternal life. Write a prayer in which you glorify Christ—give Him the honor, praise, and worship due Him as He faces the Cross.

Prayer

Do You call this glory, my Lord? I will never comprehend this thing—that You considered the Cross an honor when You could have commanded all heaven and earth to bow down before You. But though You despised the shame, this death You would embrace exalted You to heights I may never completely fathom. Let me see this, my Lord, that I might love Your glory as never before . . . the gripping glory of redeeming love.

CRUCIFY HIM!

Unfortunately, it is certain that I am also one of that crowd that doesn't give much thought to what happened. I, who am even able to write these things about the passion while remaining impassive, whereas it should only be written about in tears.

—Raniero Cantalamessa

REFLECT

Take the time to silence other sounds today—unplug the phone, put a sign on your door, turn off radios and CD players. In silence, be still and know God speaks to you. Thank Him for meeting you here day after day, never failing.

Ask God to give you the gift of a pure heart. Read the following verses slowly and thoughtfully, letting God shine His light as you evaluate:

Transgression speaks to the ungodly within his heart; there is no fear of God before his eyes. For it flatters him in his own eyes concerning the discovery of his iniquity and the hatred of it.

—Psalm 36:1–2 NASB

If we say that we have no sin, we are deceiving ourselves and the truth is not in us.

—1 John 1:8 NASB

*Because you say, "I am rich, and have become wealthy, and
have need of nothing," and you do not know that you are
wretched and miserable and poor and blind and naked.*

—Revelation 3:17 NASB

Do you hate sin? Wage war against the temptations that assail
you? Do you view yourself as one who is wretched, poor, and
needy? Purity of heart comes from a recognition and acknowl-
edgment of our need. Until we grasp our own potential for sin,
we will never fully appreciate Christ's death. Write a prayer of
commitment to seek this kind of heart based on these verses.

READ

*All the people answered, "Let his blood be on us and on
our children!"*

—Matthew 27:25 NIV

The clamorous crowd objects when Pilate appears on the
Praetorium platform alone. Throughout the morning, rumors
of the prisoner's dangerous past have spread like gangrene.
Restless ire now characterizes the growing mob, their eagerness
for execution intensifying.

"If you let Him go, you are no friend of Caesar's."

"He calls Himself a King—that makes Him an enemy of Caesar!"

Pilate watches their feigned loyalty to the Roman conqueror
with amazement. Recognizing the insanity of the farce fills him
with resentment. Yet, if word reaches Tiberius that he has
befriended an insurrectionist, his entire political career could go
up in smoke. Shaking his head, Pilate goes to retrieve the prisoner.

Within minutes Jesus stumbles onto the platform, Herod's
robe now gone. Some of the blood from the scourging has
dried, binding His tunic to His back. His face, though bloated
and bruised, looks pasty white, His eyes nearly swollen shut.

What must the Christ be thinking now? Does He drift in and
out of consciousness, barely aware of the noisy chatter below?

Does He dream of a seraph coming to cool His brow or bind His broken body?

Judgment is nigh for the One who will one day judge the world. What does He think of these accusers who stand before Him this day as judge and jury? What does Jesus feel for the procurator who persists in proclaiming His innocence but lacks the courage to make the right choice?

Taking his official seat on the platform, Pilate orders the soldiers to bring the prisoner forward for sentencing. The late morning sun beats down, and a servant hurries to hold an umbrella over Pilate's head. No shade is offered the Christ, who leans weakly against a soldier's arm.

"Here is your King!" Pilate taunts the religious leaders.

"Take Him away. Crucify Him!" they cry back.

"What? Shall I crucify your King?"

"We have no king but Caesar," one priest calls out, the crowd chiming in with a chant-like drone.

Pilate, astonished at their fervor, motions to a guard. The noise dies down as he sets a basin of water before him. Reaching into the bowl, the procurator rinses his hands slowly and methodically as if practicing some ancient ritual. Finally he looks up and announces with authority: "I am innocent of the blood of this righteous Man. See to it yourselves."

"His blood shall be on us and on our children!" a high priest shouts. Making a mantra of the sacred words, priest after priest affirms his own willingness to assume responsibility for Christ's punishment. As His accusers the law requires nothing less, but in this moment when doubts would seem reasonable, they relish instead their role as witnesses for the prosecution.

His blood shall be on us and on our children! The dreadful sound slices through the air like another blow assaulting Jesus the Christ. These who pride themselves in teaching others the ways of God can't possibly comprehend the eternal significance of the words they speak.

For it is not this sham of a trial that sends Jesus to Calvary, but a people who've fallen short of God's glory. No human being can ever wash their hands of Him, but the blood He sheds there fills a fountain where all may plunge, losing their guilty stains. *His blood be on us and on our children,* for it has the power to heal an eternity of hell within our hearts.

RESPOND

Hear the words like a chant in your own ears: *His blood be on us and on our children.* What must Jesus have felt when the sound of it filled the air? What might He have wanted to say?

Consider the punishment Jesus is about to undergo. See yourself as morally responsible. Say quietly, "Your blood is upon me . . . Jesus."

Read the following verses aloud as a prayer of worship and gratitude:

Your lovingkindness, O LORD, extends to the heavens, Your faithfulness reaches to the skies. Your righteousness is like the mountains of God; Your judgments are like a great deep. O LORD, You preserve man and beast. How precious is Your lovingkindness, O God! And the children of men take refuge in the shadow of Your wings. They drink their fill of the abundance of Your house; and You give them to drink of the river of Your delights.
—Psalm 36:5–8 NASB

PRAYER

Oh, Lord, Your blood is on me and my children. I say it with shame. I cannot even look into Your eyes, for the sadness there reopens the wounds of my sinful heart and like an infected sore, they ooze with sordid filth. But I must look—I must, for through the sorrow You invite me to come and be cleansed. And so I will. Let Your blood be on me and in me and over me, and I will be pure, whiter than snow, precious Redeemer.

18 SENTENCED

> *Thorns, it seems, always accompany visits to glory. No one who has walked in Christ's presence will ever be allowed to strut.*
>
> —Jamie Buckingham

REFLECT

Rejoice today that God is here. Turn your thoughts toward Him, asking that He reveal Himself to you in a unique way through this time with Him.

Hundreds of years before Christ was sentenced to die on Calvary, Isaiah prophesied of the Passion, saying:

> *Just as many were astonished at you, My people, so His appearance was marred more than any man and His form more than the sons of men.*
>
> —Isaiah 52:14 NASB

Read this verse again as you prepare your heart to see its fulfillment in today's reading.

Read (or sing) the words to the following old hymn meditatively, offering them as your own prayer to the Lord.

O Sacred Head, Now Wounded
Bernard of Clairvaux

*O sacred Head, now wounded, with grief and shame
weighed down,*

*Now scornfully surrounded with thorns Your only
  crown,
O sacred Head, no glory now from Your face does shine;
Yet, though despised and gory, I joy to call You mine.*

*Men mock and taunt and jeer You. They smite Your
  countenance.
Though mighty worlds shall fear You, and flee before
  Your glance.
How pale You are with anguish, with sore abuse and
  scorn!
Your eyes with pain now languish that once were bright
  as morn!*

*My burden in Your passion, Lord, You have borne for
  me,
For it was my transgression, my shame, on Calvary.
I cast me down before you; wrath is my rightful lot.
Have mercy, I implore You; Redeemer, spurn me not!*

*What language shall I borrow to thank You, dearest
  Friend,
For this, Your dying sorrow, Your pity without end?
Oh, make me Yours forever, and keep me strong and
  true;
Lord, let me never, never outlive my love for You.*

READ

They began to acclaim Him, "Hail, King of the Jews!"
                              —Mark 15:18 NASB

Pilate watches the crowd with disgusted resignation. How he
deplores giving them their way. But better the head of this
eccentric Jew than his own. Out of options, he summons a centurion, mouthing terse orders.

The cries for crucifixion continue to rise sporadically from various factions. Jesus sways to one side. He appears to be on the verge of passing out.

The centurion returns holding the arm of Barabbas. Pilate declares his official release, and the crowd cheers as he reunites with his fellow revolutionaries below. Meanwhile, the soldiers flanking Jesus pull Him along to the palace courtyard. Breathing a collective sigh of relief, the priests and elders believe at last that execution is inevitable.

The crowd begins to break up. Some head to the temple for worship, while others move to the marketplace to buy unleavened bread for the day's meal. Many remain, waiting for the prisoner to be led out to the place called Golgotha.

Inside the courtyard, hundreds of soldiers are forming rows in military precision to prepare for the imminent death march. Those close to Jesus of Nazareth are taken aback at His condition. What a pitiful sight—one more man with a messiah complex. How could He have ever made any claim to royalty? What would make Him dream such dreams?

A few joke at the absurdity of the whole thing. One soldier grabs a thin branch covered with long, hard thorns from a pile of firewood nearby, and begins to weave it into a wreath to crown the would-be king.

Seeing them, a captain from the Italian regiment takes off his military robe. With dramatic flair he drapes it across Jesus' shoulders, bowing deeply as he backs away. One by one others pick up the revelry, laughing and taunting the Christ. Finished with his crown, the soldier stands back and admires his artwork, placing it on Jesus' head to mimic an official coronation.

"Hail, King of the Jews!" he cries out jovially. Others crowd around, fawning over Jesus as they drop to their knees and salute sarcastically with words of cheer.

"Godspeed, O mighty one!"

"Rejoice, O great ruler!"

Hail, King of the Jews! A centurion calls out: "His scepter— He is a king; He must have a scepter!"

Someone grabs one of the branches from the pile and places it in Jesus' right hand. He is so very alone now. What must He feel in this crowd? At least His own people, though they knew Him not, expectantly awaited the Messiah foretold in sacred Scripture. Whether they loved or hated Him, Jesus' claims were always taken seriously.

But these Gentiles—have they ever wanted a Savior? Or does the power they hold rob them of any sense of their need? When Jesus looks at them does He see the frailty behind their pride? In the mocking faces, does He see some who will one day follow Him? Does He gaze into the eyes of a Cornelius and secretly rejoice at what he will be, once the price has been paid for his sins?

The blood drips down into His eyes and across His face, the makeshift crown slipping from His matted hair. Someone grabs a branch and hits at it, embedding the barbs in His skull. Lust for blood spurs other soldiers to join in pounding Jesus' head with reeds.

Soon their abuse grows to a feverish pitch. One squares off, slaps Jesus, and spits in His face. A few others follow suit. The fun and games have become a sadistic sport, with Jesus the impotent victim.

Hail, King of the Jews! Crowned with thorns, the King of kings finally faces death's mournful march. Eternal darkness looms over the One to whom every eye will one day look, though for now His battered face is repulsive to see. Weak and powerless, the Son of God advances toward a host of hell's demons to wage the final war for the souls of men.

RESPOND

The walk to Golgotha is almost here. Consider the emotions Jesus must face at this moment. Think of His physical state. Contemplate the mockery that He faced from the Romans. See this scene before you, and then read the following description of the exalted Messiah, Jesus Christ:

I saw one like a son of man, clothed in a robe reaching to the feet, and girded across His chest with a golden sash. His head and His hair were white like white wool, like snow; and His eyes were like a flame of fire. His feet were like burnished bronze, when it has been made to glow in a furnace, and His voice was like the sound of many waters. In His right hand He held seven stars, and out of His mouth came a sharp two-edged sword; and His face was like the sun shining in its strength. When I saw Him, I fell at His feet like a dead man.

—Revelation 1:13–17 NASB

Consider the contrast. Reflect on what Jesus endured in light of the reality of His Deity. Write a prayer of adoration based on these thoughts, using 2 Corinthians 8:9 as a basis: "For you know the grace of our Lord Jesus Christ, that though He was rich, yet for your sake He became poor, so that you through His poverty might become rich" (NASB).

Spend some time in quiet contemplation of these things.

PRAYER

Oh, my Lord of lords—You whose head should bear only crowns of gold are wreathed with nasty thorns. You who should be hailed as matchless King are ridiculed with sarcasm. You whose heavenly anthem should drown all other sounds are deluged with derisive taunts. Every melody of love loses its luster in light of this haunting song Your soul must now sing. How can a sinner such as I ever join the chorus?

CALVARY

I heard it again recently—a preacher insisting that *our* God doesn't hang from a cross. He is risen! This subtle minimizing of Christ's death characterized my evangelical upbringing. We wouldn't think of wearing a crucifix, never attended Good Friday services, and took Communion once a month on Sunday nights when the crowds were small. We didn't ignore the Crucifixion but seemed bent on giving it second billing. In the process, I believe we missed out on abundant treasures of the faith.

Jesus walked in penetrating awareness of His death. He described details of it to His disciples three times and alluded to it often. He used His final meal as an object lesson on the significance of what He was about to do.

The Gospels cover Christ's death extensively—almost half of John's story is of Jesus' final hours. Paul's letters champion a crucified Christ, boldly making this the centerpiece of his faith. Peter points to the way in which Jesus died as the supreme example of how we are to live on earth.

John's vision of eternity in the book of Revelation reminds us that heaven will be a continual exaltation of Christ crucified. Referring to Jesus as the *Lamb* twenty-seven times, he unfolds a glorious picture of the *Lamb that was slain* seated on the throne, surrounded by worshipers from every tribe and tongue.

I cherish Easter celebrations for their joyfulness. But before we embrace resurrection life, let us linger a little longer with Christ in death. Let us travel the Via Dolorosa and experience the wondrous mystery that before Jesus burst from the grave to prove His power, He laid down His life and poured out His love.

19 LED AWAY

*At the head of the procession of life, then,
is a thorn-crowned Man, his pains healing
our pains, his wounds answering our
wounds, his love taking our sin.*

—Earl Stanley Jones

REFLECT

Today the walk up Calvary begins, and it is important to prepare for God's voice. Contemplating the Cross can be emotional, spiritual, and even physical. Ask God to help you focus, letting other cares dissipate in light of the love you will see. Be quiet in His presence for a few minutes.

Read the following prayer (taken from *The Book of Common Worship*, Presbyterian Church), offering each phrase from your own heart to the Lord for this time.

Forbid, O God, that we should forget, amid our earthly comforts, the pains and mortal anguish that our Lord Jesus endured for our salvation. Grant us this day a true vision of all that He suffered, in His betrayal, His lonely agony, His false trial, His mocking and scourging, and the torture of death upon the cross. As Thou hast given Thyself utterly for us, may we give ourselves entirely to Thee, O Jesus Christ, our only Lord and Savior. Amen.

READ

They led Him out to crucify Him.
—Mark 15:20 NASB

A sudden hush falls over the courtyard as Pilate enters with his entourage. The prisoner, sickly and silent, stares blankly at the ground. Rivulets of blood from the thorny wreath drip down His face, and there are new bruises where the soldiers hit Him with reeds.

Pilate grimaces at what he sees. The centurion in charge, only slightly embarrassed at his men's crass behavior, strips Jesus of the cloak used to mock Him moments ago. Feeling Pilate's rage, he barks orders for his men to bring the other prisoners out and prepare for the crucifixions.

Just then, three soldiers enter the courtyard, each carrying a wooden plank. Weighing almost one hundred pounds and measuring six feet long, the beams are an ominous reminder that Rome's most grueling form of execution will soon take place.

Can Jesus even lift His head? The effects of the scourging alone could claim His life here in the courtyard. What strength of will is required for Him to fight these throes of death? Given the horror of the price He must yet pay, what keeps Him from letting go and embracing the end right now?

The men place the heavy beam across Jesus' left shoulder. Bringing His arms up around it, they tie each hand to the wood so it cannot drop on the road to Golgotha. The massive weight against the open wounds on His back causes Him to hunch over in anguish. Each attempt to straighten back up brings even greater pain as the rough wood rubs His raw flesh. How much more can one body endure?

The presiding officer motions to the soldiers. Jesus, pushed to the front and flanked on all sides by men from the Roman army, moves through the arches of the palace courtyard and into the street. Several priests and elders wait to accompany the procession. Families line the narrow road that will take the prisoner away from town to the foot of Golgotha.

Jesus' eyes blink in the glaring sun as He tries to survey the streets of Jerusalem one last time. In the marketplace, men and women conduct the business of life, and boys and girls play merrily as if it were any other day. The journey that began in the heart of His Father, before the foundation of the earth, has only 650 yards to go. Yet for this One whose body screams in pain with every step, it spans an eternity of torment whose end cannot even be fathomed.

Respond

Sit very still, listening to the sounds of Jerusalem—the busy marketplace, the hustle and bustle of ordinary life. Hear the sounds of your own world today—phones, traffic, radios, televisions, talking and laughing. Now, in your mind, freeze-frame these two scenes side by side. In the middle of them, see Jesus, beaten, barely able to move, bent under the weight of the crossbeam. Sense the significance of a world that goes on, oblivious to the reality of a living sacrifice being led to the slaughter on their behalf.

Consider the days of your own life when you are unaware, insensitive to Christ's journey to the cross, to the extreme price He paid for you—for you. Contemplate the kind of love that gives and gives, even in the face of apparent indifference. Respond with worship, tears, repentance, or rejoicing.

Write a prayer beginning with these words: *Lord Jesus, You walk today and every day to Calvary, while I . . .*

Prayer

Lord Jesus, You walk today and every day to Calvary, while I make beds and drive carpools. You bleed, wounds festering, body failing, while I pay bills and play tennis. You trudge along, one lonely step after another, while I make phone calls and go shopping. Lord Jesus, You walk today and every day to Calvary for me—grant that this thought will crash through my callous oblivion, piercing my busyness with pangs of brokenhearted love.

20 VIA DOLOROSA

> *When we look at his cross, we understand*
> *his love. His head is bent down to kiss us.*
> *His hands are extended to embrace us. His*
> *heart is wide open to receive us.*
>
> —Saint Augustine

REFLECT

Come in deep reverence to spend time in God's presence today. Gently open your heart—see yourself taking off your shoes to enter the holy of holies, where God will speak to you.

Read the following verses as a prayer back to Christ:

> *He is the image of the invisible God, the firstborn of all creation. For by Him all things were created, both in the heavens and on earth, visible and invisible, whether thrones or dominions or rulers or authorities—all things have been created through Him and for Him. He is before all things, and in Him all things hold together.*
>
> —Colossians 1:15–17 NASB

Ponder these realities about the exalted Lord as you encounter this same Jesus on the Via Dolorosa—the "way of suffering"—today.

READ

> *They took Jesus, therefore, and He went out, bearing His own cross.*
>
> —John 19:17 NASB

Conducting crucifixions is no easy task in this city whose population swells every year for Passover with tens of thousands of worshiping pilgrims. The road is narrow, making the soldiers' job of clearing the streets for the procession nigh impossible. The jostling about causes Jesus to grimace, His strength waning with each step.

The other two prisoners, much stronger for not having been beaten or scourged, are pressed ahead of Him. Still, Jesus must stop often. Feet blistering from the sun-scorched road, He can scarcely catch His breath through the searing pain. Fever infuses His flesh. He lurches forward. Dazed and almost delirious, His body finally collapses facedown in the dirt.

Arms askew, the crossbeam lands heavily on His shoulders, pinning Him to the ground. To those watching the pitiful scene, it appears He may have died. Word passes up the line and the centurion halts the procession. Hurrying back to the place where Jesus lies, he surveys the crowd.

"You there—yes, you. Come here."

Simon, a large man from Cyrene in North Africa, steps back, hoping they don't mean him. Having just come in from the country to take his sons to the temple, he tries to turn and be on his way.

"You—I said you—come take this stake and carry it to Golgotha."

With these words an ordinary father, a preoccupied pilgrim, is pressed into service for the Savior of the world. Does irritation at Rome's invasion of privacy stir within him? Does he feel for this fellow Jew who's been treated with such cruelty? Does he have any idea how this single event will impact history? Will Passover ever be the same for Simon the Cyrene?

Soldiers untie the beam from Jesus' wrists and pass it to Simon. Fearful that the prisoner will die before the official execution, the captain of the guard leans down to pull Jesus gently to His feet. Staggering, He opens His eyes.

A distant sound breaks through the stillness that has surrounded the scene at Jerusalem's gates. As the group moves out, it grows louder. The cries are chilling—women with no self-control weeping and wailing for the One who cannot carry His own cross.

Who are they? Professional mourners given the task of lamenting the death of those who face crucifixion? Women whose husbands once left them behind to join the radical Rabbi's movement? Friends of the victim's mother, Mary? Or women who perhaps not long ago found compassion in the eyes of this One now condemned to death?

As the procession draws near the mournful dirge, Jesus stops and looks into the crowd. A tear runs from one blue-black eye down His face. From deep within He summons a strange stamina and speaks with the authority of a prophet: "Daughters of Jerusalem, don't weep for Me. Weep for yourselves and for your children."

The crowd is hushed, tear-stained faces bewildered at Jesus' sudden burst of energy. He continues: "A time is coming when you will believe that it is a blessed thing to be barren, to never have had children in this evil world."

The women murmur among themselves. What is He saying? Empty wombs are the curse of Jewish women. How could that ever be a blessing?

Scanning their faces, Jesus goes on. "You will beg the mountains to fall and crush you and the hills to cover you completely. For if these things happen to a green tree, what will happen to those that are dry?"

Soldiers weave through the crowd, trying to break it up as they press the prisoner forward. What an odd turn of events. A few seconds ago this Man collapsed under His own crossbeam. Now He stands strong, admonishing the crowd with words none of them seem to understand.

Even in the throes of agony, Jesus seems compelled to warn men and women of the wrath to come. What kind of yearning fills His heart? Does He see those who will reject His offer of salvation, even after He has paid such a price? Does He feel for some who mourn now, but will never truly repent? In this moment, does He intercede to the Father for ones such as these?

And the march moves on. Jesus, who for one brief spell forgot His pain, winces again with every step. As they pass through a nondescript neighborhood, people watch the spectacle from their rooftops, calling out their own opinions of His innocence or guilt. Pharisees with their phylacteries containing the sacred words of Scripture flank the procession on either side. And the living Word of God moves outside city gates, with only a hill left to climb.

RESPOND

Place yourself in the streets of Jerusalem that day. When Jesus falls, would you gladly carry His cross? Would your heart break with the women's? What would you do as He passes by? Wipe His face with a cool cloth? Offer Him a drink of pure water? Look into His pain-racked eyes and tell Him you are sorry He suffers so?

Spend some time contemplating this, then offer your response to Him. Try to tell Him how you feel this moment, and what you would do to change things if you could.

PRAYER

Oh, God, I am deeply mourning today. I want to wail at what they have done to You, to weep gut-wrenching sobs over Your mutilated back and pummeled face. I want to stop the whole thing and make it go away. I want to have never been the reason for Your journey down Via Dolorosa. How foolish the thought. For I have sinned and it is the weight of this—not a wooden beam—that hurls You to the ground. I mourn, for what else can I do?

 **21** GOLGOTHA

I want to recover the truth that Jesus was not crucified on an altar between two candlesticks, but on a garbage heap at a crossroads of the world . . . where soldiers gambled and cynics talked smut.

—George McCloud

REFLECT

Sit in hushed silence with God today, enjoying Him, relishing these moments as precious gifts to you and blessings to Him. There is sorrow in the Cross, but also great joy. The anticipation of joy is what enabled Jesus to endure the horror of Calvary. Read the following poem slowly and offer it as a prayer (or give your own) to the Lord, based on the joy you sense as you consider the Cross today:

How Splendid the Cross

How splendid the cross of Christ!
It brings life, not death;
Light, not darkness;
Paradise, not its loss.
It is the wood on which the Lord, like a great warrior,
was wounded in hands and feet and side,
but healed thereby our wounds.
A tree had destroyed us;
a tree now brought us life.
　　　—Saint Theodore of Studios, *Breakfast with the Saints*

READ

> *They brought Him to the place Golgotha, which is translated, Place of a Skull.*
>
> —Mark 15:22 NASB

The small hill outside the Gennath Gate in Jerusalem buzzes with activity. The other two criminals begin their ascent while Jesus lingers at the bottom, trying to muster enough strength for the short climb.

Two major roads intersect at the base of Golgotha. Merchants from the port of Joppa in the west, and travelers from Samaria and even farther south, have a clear view up the fifteen-foot slope as they enter the city.

Crucifixion has proved an effective deterrent to crime for the Roman government. On any given day, a number of beams bearing the bodies of the accused proclaim to the passing masses that a vile death awaits those who break their laws.

Golgotha—Place of a Skull—has garnered a reputation far and wide. No one knows how it got its name, but stories abound. Some say it simply looks like a skull, with two caverns for eyes and a large jutting rock formation for a nose. Others believe it earned the name from the thousands of criminals who have been executed here. Whatever one might think, the mount outside the city gate is worthy of its title. It is a symbol of death to all whose lives it touches.

Soldiers shout at those crowding the busy crossroads, eager to get their prisoner up the narrow path. Every step Jesus takes inflicts pain beyond comprehension. Centurions now hold His arms on either side, gently guiding Him forward.

Passersby who happen to be in the wrong place at the wrong time hurry away, quickly covering their children's eyes at the gruesome sight of the condemned. Those who have followed since the trial at Fortress Antonia jostle and push ahead, determined to find a place at the foot of the three beams.

What occupies the mind of Christ as He faces the final steps to His death? Does dread eat at His resolve? Does fear cause His heart to pound and His stomach to heave? Does He long to draw on His divinity to infuse strength into His broken body?

As they reach the top, a soldier orders Simeon to drop the crossbeam. Another moves toward Jesus, handing Him a metal cup. How thirsty He must be. Has He had so much as a sip of water since His arrest in Gethsemane? The offer must seem like a gift, a respite from the onslaught within and without.

What does He think as He holds the cup in His hands? Does it remind Him that only hours ago He held another, pleading for it to pass? This cup holds sour wine mixed with myrrh, an analgesic to deaden His senses and ease the pain. As He lifts it to His swollen lips, does He remember the bitter taste of sin from the cup He resisted so in the Garden?

The soldiers are unsure what to do when Jesus hands the cup back after barely tasting the foul potion. Their leaders prefer civilized executions, and without sedation crucified criminals often scream in agony. Never before has anyone refused to drink the drug. The soldier who poured the wine shrugs and tosses out the contents. Does Jesus consider that even now He could dash the cup of man's sin to the ground like the sticky wine on the grass at His feet?

For hundreds of years sacrifices have been offered for sin— the blood of animals sprinkled across altars and their rank carcasses burned outside the camp. Soon the stench of Jesus' flesh will waft through the air outside Jerusalem's gates. But first, the blood of the Lamb must be spilled on this altar that was fashioned before the foundation of the world.

RESPOND

In your own mind, stand at the top of Mount Calvary. See the crowds coming and going below. See the massive temple and the beautiful city of Jerusalem. Hear the conversations of those who have come up the hill. Watch Jesus take the final steps to the top. Imagine His emotions, thoughts, and fears.

Carefully consider the following verses:

For the bodies of those animals whose blood is brought into the holy place by the high priest as an offering for sin, are burned outside the camp. Therefore Jesus also, that He might sanctify the people through His own blood, suffered outside the gate. So, let us go out to Him outside the camp, bearing His reproach.

—Hebrews 13:11–13 NASB

See Jesus suffering outside the gate of Jerusalem. Go to Him, bearing (figuratively carrying) His reproach (suffering, reviling, upbraiding). This simply means to feel within and have a deep appreciation for all He endured, willing to suffer yourself if it will further His kingdom.

After a while, write a few words expressing your thoughts and compassion to Christ.

PRAYER

Lord, You who own the cattle on a thousand hills now suffer reproach on one of them. The scent of Your sacrifice is a stench in the nostrils of those who do not understand, those who look the other way, those who clutch their rebellion to their blackened hearts. But to me, Lord, it is sweet—sometimes too strong for my sinful soul—but sweet nonetheless. Help me to breathe deeply that Your aroma of death might finally permeate my heart of hearts.

22   NAILED TO A CROSS

If we men and women of this latter day wish to gaze into the awfulness of sin, we shall have to take our stand at the mystic confluence of midnight and noonday and abide in the cross of our Lord Jesus Christ.
—Warren Wiersbe

REFLECT

Set your heart toward God today. Acknowledge His presence with you, thanking Him for His faithfulness. Ask Him to give you a tenderness toward His Son in these final hours.

Jesus made an amazing promise concerning His death:

I, if I am lifted up from the earth, will draw all men to Myself.
—John 12:32 NASB

Consider this truth as you focus on Jesus being lifted up to die in today's narrative. Stop at times while you are reading and speak this verse aloud, offering a heart of gratitude that because He died, you have been drawn to Him.

READ

When they came to the place called The Skull, there they crucified Him.
—Luke 23:33 NASB

The four soldiers assigned to the prisoner named Jesus move quickly into action. First, they strip Him of His clothing. When they reach the inner garments, blood and flesh tear from wounds already festering with grisly infection. Jesus' eyes roll back in His head in agony. The Crucifixion has begun.

Women turn their heads in shame at the sight of His bare body. The extent of His wounds shocks even soldiers who tend to take their task of execution lightly. One grabs the loincloth and begins to wrap it around Jesus' waist and through His legs. If He were a Gentile, He would be hung naked. It is a small concession to the Hebrew people whose sacred beliefs abhor nudity. When they finish, they lead Jesus over to the cross-beam, instructing Him to lie down and place His arms out across the rough wood.

Sometimes prisoners resist and have to be shoved to the ground, head banging on the wood. But Jesus responds with perplexing submission. His head falls back, the crown of thorns pressing deeper into His skull. Mustering His strength, He rises up level with the crossbeam. Dust and small pebbles cling to the open wounds on His back and legs.

What must it be like for the Son of God to finally lay down His life? How does it feel to stretch His arms out on the cross-beam of crucifixion? Does He hold on to this moment for which He entered the human race? Can He see the joy of victory somewhere in the vast expanse of eternity?

One soldier puts Jesus' right arm in place. The other positions the tip of an iron spike, five inches long and almost a half-inch across, in the middle of His wrist. An expert in the art of crucifixion, the soldier lifts his hammer and with one strike embeds the nail through the flesh into the wood. The pinging thud echoes across the hill as the crowd watches.

When just a trickle of blood appears, the soldier nods, relieved that he hasn't severed any main arteries. To do so would bring about a quick death. The longer it takes, the greater the suffering, and the more likely people will see and be cowed into fearful allegiance to the Roman government.

The spike crushes numerous nerve endings, and Jesus moans. Bolts of pain shoot down the length of His arm. Before He can catch His breath, they extend His left arm. The sound of hammer against iron rings again in the ears of onlookers. Now pain radiates through both arms, up His neck, through His ears and eyes until it feels as if His head might explode.

When they are done the centurion gives the signal and they lift the wood above their heads, suspending Jesus in midair. The other two soldiers place forked poles under the beam, carrying it toward the empty stipe. The weight of Christ's body pulls on His wrists. Each fraction of movement wrenches Him, sometimes swinging His torso forward. Every wound inflicted up till now fades in proportion to this.

A lettered piece of wood identifying Jesus and His crime hangs on the center stipe. The soldiers push their poles until the crossbeam snaps into place under the words. Jesus presses His feet against the wood, trying to lift Himself from the suffocating grip of the cross.

Taking hold of His left foot, a soldier places it on top of the right, pressing them down to drive the final nail through Jesus' arches. Though once again little blood is shed, an intense ache grips the muscles in Jesus' legs. He now hangs between two criminals only a few feet from the ground. The soldier's job is done, and those left to watch settle in for the long wait.

Does Jesus close His eyes, focusing on the time He'll be freed from His broken body to return to His Father? Does the agony in His feet remind Him of the enemy whose head He will soon bruise? Does He look out at those who watch, making mental note of who has come and who has not come to His crucifixion? Or does He scan the vast city of Jerusalem and beyond, grieving once again such spiritual poverty?

The Son of Man is lifted up and thereby will one day draw all men to Himself. But for now, searing spasms in His arms and legs are a tortuous reminder that death is not easy and will not come quickly. There are battles yet to fight, victories not quite won, and a price not yet paid for the sins of a dying world.

Respond

Contemplate this moment when Jesus is raised up on a cross to die. Consider all He has been through up to this point in preparation for it. Spend a few minutes thinking about each of the three nails as they go into His flesh. Try to comprehend what He may have experienced as the crossbeam was attached to the stipe.

Beyond the physical agony, consider that few were there to support Him. Other than Peter, who betrayed him, and John, who now stands near—His closest friends have not shown their faces since Gethsemane. Also, ponder the shame of a crucifixion where friend and foe and stranger watch you, knowing the crime you are condemned for. When you feel you can identify in some small way with Christ as He is lifted up, write a prayer, a poem, a meditation, a thought to express your heart to Him.

Prayer

Jesus, my Jesus hanging in the wind, sun burning, body bare save for a loincloth and wounds too many to count. I wonder why You hold on to life amid Golgotha's death grip. You said that if You were lifted up You'd draw all men to You. Is this what You meant? To be lifted up like this? The perplexity of such a plan plagues me still. Yet You hang there and I am irresistibly drawn to Your side. I cannot turn away—not now, not ever.

CRUCIFIXION

He was an unlikely evangelist, a superstar whose rakish good looks and action thrillers had garnered worldwide acclaim for decades. His project was an improbable one—a film most felt destined for failure. But the idea for it had burned like a fire in his belly until it became the movie that he said "he couldn't *not* make." Defying the naysayers, Mel Gibson directed, produced, and distributed *The Passion of the Christ*, a disturbing, graphic portrayal of Jesus' suffering and death.

Who could have predicted the furor that would ensue? Critics both panned and lauded its release, while most of the entertainment industry scorned it. Christian leaders praised its gospel message, even as charges of gratuitous violence and anti-Semitism ran rampant. The only thing everyone seemed to agree on was that this film would not leave you ambivalent.

And so it has ever been. Though broadly embraced as a religious icon, the cross—when shown for what it really is—descends like a brooding storm, ominous, unsettling. While there have always been travelers on that narrow road who have found in Christ's passion the means to save their souls, most regard any notion of their need for redemption as foolishness.

Gibson's "folly" had sprung from the smoldering ruins of a holocaust in his own soul some ten years earlier. Drawn to the Crucifixion, he found himself wrestling with Christ's wounds until they became a balm for his tormented heart. In the process, he was made new.

As we contemplate these final moments of Christ's passion, let us pray that God's Spirit will perform such a miracle of grace upon our hearts. Then, let us bow down and worship His majesty.

23   Forgiveness

What do you weep at, if you do not weep at this?

—Dante Alighieri

Reflect

The next several days will be spent at the foot of Jesus' cross. Make sure you have enough time, and a quiet place to focus. Rest in the compassionate presence of God, who loves you and gives His life for you. Softly, slowly speak or sing the words to the following old hymn:

And Can It Be That I Should Gain?
Charles Wesley

*And can it be that I should gain
An interest in the Savior's blood?
Died He for me, who caused His pain?
For me, who Him to death pursued?
Amazing love! how can it be
That Thou, my God, shouldst die for me?*

*He left His Father's throne above,
So free, so infinite His grace!
Emptied Himself of all but love,
And bled for Adam's helpless race!
'Tis mercy all, immense and free,
For, O my God, it found out me.*

Amazing love! how can it be
That Thou, my God, shouldst die for me?

READ

Jesus was saying, "Father, forgive them; for they do not
know what they are doing."
—Luke 23:34 NASB

The hustle and bustle of life goes on below the crucifixion mount. Though travelers stop now and then to stare inquisitively, the bodies hanging there are a disturbing sight, and most hurry on to their business within the city.

Those who've come to watch the crucifixions form an eclectic group—religious leaders with righteous resolve, soldiers there to do a job, and curious onlookers who hope for some entertainment from this One rumored to possess magical powers.

There is another group, separate from the rest. One man and a handful of women huddle a short way from the center cross in stoic silence, grief covering their tear-streaked faces. Some recognize John as a follower of Jesus, his arm around an older woman who cannot take her swollen eyes from the scene before her.

Jesus, now flushed with fever, feels suffocation closing in like a vise as He gasps for breath. Raising Himself up on His feet to exhale and relieve the constriction in His chest, He is jolted by sharp pains shooting through His calves and within seconds must drop down again.

The soldiers, calloused from exposure to a thousand days like this one, look for ways to occupy the time. Sporadic laughter erupts as they entertain one another with coarse jokes. Those in charge of the Crucifixion flank the three crosses. They must stay to the end, making sure no one takes a body down before proof of death.

One of them notices the pile of clothing on the ground at Jesus' feet. Calling to the others, he asks how they want to divide it. They examine each piece, shaking their heads. Not much worth having this time—bloody stains have ruined most of it. Someone must have removed the head covering during the scourging, for it alone appears unsoiled.

The captain quickly claims it for himself while the others haggle over the rest. One takes the worn sandals, another the girdle, and a third the robe. The only thing left is the inner tunic. It is so saturated with blood that one cannot see the original color. Someone suggests they divide it into four parts—the only fair way to dispose of the fifth piece of clothing, worthless though it might be.

Trying to find a good place to tear it, they soon realize there are no seams. Turning it over and over, they are amazed. Superstitious and fearful of the strange garment, no one wants to bother with it. They pass the crusty cloth around, finally deciding its fate through a guessing game with their fingers. The winner tosses the seamless tunic aside.

Above the revelry the three condemned to die hang silently, save an occasional groan or cry from one of the robbers. Jesus does not make a sound. The soldiers look them over, and satisfied that death is not imminent, take their positions once again.

"Father, forgive them; for they do not know what they are doing." Those near the cross are startled by the voice of the One hanging in the center. What a strange thing to say. Who tugs at Jesus' heartstrings this moment? Cold and calculating soldiers who have no idea that He may one day save their souls? Stony-hearted priests and elders who've made an idol of their rules and abandoned the living God? Passersby whose lives are so empty they find diversion in the horror of a crucifixion?

Some draw closer as if they hope to hear Him a little better. It is difficult to read the expression on Jesus' face after having uttered His first words from the cross. A gentle anguish seems to cloud His eyes. Seven times Jesus will find the fortitude to lift Himself and speak cryptic words as He hangs from the cross. But this first utterance reflects a depth of compassion beyond human understanding.

Father, forgive them; for they do not know what they are doing.

In the unseen realm, God the Father gently nods His head, and angels' hearts break at such amazing love.

Respond

Close your eyes to experience this moment at the cross. See the soldiers laugh and joke as they divide Jesus' clothes. Smell the sweat in the air as the morning sun burns down. Hear the rumble of conversation among the high priests. Look at Jesus hanging there. See His eyes on you. Hear Him say, "Father, forgive," for every act of sin, rebellion, apathy, or disobedience you have ever committed or will commit.

Read the following verse, very slowly: "God demonstrates His own love toward us, in that while we were yet sinners, Christ died for us" (Romans 5:8 NASB). Worship God and thank Him. Write a prayer based on this truth.

Prayer

Dearest Savior, I hear Your voice breaking through the heat of a summer morning and the busyness of my days. I am back there—standing at Your feet with heartless soldiers and hardhearted priests. I, too, have sealed Your fate with my sins and am in desperate need of compassion. So tenderly You offer forgiveness to them . . . to the world . . . to me. Your voice descends like a gentle rain on the desert of my heart until I am soft and pliable in Your nail-pierced hands.

24 KING OF THE JEWS

Behold what great contempt hath the Lord of Majesty endured, that his confusion may be our glory; his punishment our heavenly bliss! Without ceasing impress this spectacle, O Christian, on thy soul!

—Dionysius

REFLECT

Come to God's throne today in reverence and awe for the power He holds over all things. Affirm His right to be Lord over your own life. Humble yourself before Him, asking Him to purify you from sin. Thank Him for the price He paid that you can come boldly into His throne-room.

Read the following excerpts from Psalm 29 aloud as a praise to the King of kings:

Ascribe to the LORD, O sons of the mighty, ascribe to the LORD glory and strength. Ascribe to the LORD the glory due to His name; worship the LORD in holy array. The voice of the LORD is upon the waters; the God of glory thunders, the LORD is over many waters. The voice of the LORD is powerful, the voice of the LORD is majestic . . . The voice of the LORD makes the deer to calve and strips the forests bare; and in His temple everything says, "Glory!" The LORD sat as King at the flood; yes, the LORD sits as King forever.

—Psalm 29:1–4, 9–10 NASB

Write a prayer of worship and exaltation, personalizing His status in your own life.

READ

Above His head they put up the charge against Him which read, "THIS IS JESUS THE KING OF THE JEWS."
—Matthew 27:37 NASB

For a moment, Golgotha is quiet. Soldiers close their eyes for a morning nap, while onlookers converse in whispers, wondering how long they'll have to wait for the condemned to take their final breaths. John and the women watch Jesus' face, hoping for some sign that His suffering is coming to an end.

Jesus presses His feet together, digging His toes into the wood to lift Himself up again. He spews out air, then gasps like a drowning swimmer who knows he is about to go under. His battered face has taken on a purplish hue, making Him look grotesque and surreal. It is almost impossible to recognize Him.

He drops back down, His face contorting with pain as the weight of His body drags on His weak arms. The inscription above His head is now smeared with blood, yet the words written in three languages can be clearly seen, even by those on the road below. *This is Jesus the King of the Jews.*

These are sacred words, written in the language of the Hebrew Torah. They are powerful words, written in the language of the Roman conqueror Caesar. And they are universal words, written in Greek, the language that will soon record the gospel of Christ for all the world and every generation to come.

The significance of the title has not been lost on Caiaphas, the chief priest. Confident that he has destroyed Jesus' influence in life, he now fears what might come of a martyr's death. Furious that Pilate would encourage such a thing by giving Jesus of Nazareth this epithet, he has sent a group to demand that the wording be changed.

The number of priests and elders on the mount has dwindled. Those that remain hover anxiously, talking among themselves. Watching Caiaphas seethe, they wonder what will happen if his demand is not met.

The return of the three priests breaks the stillness on the mount. Their visit has not been successful. Quickly they tell their story to the others. First they had demanded Christ's real crime of treason be listed on the sign with His name.

Shocked at Pilate's refusal, they regrouped, finally insisting that he at least add the words "He said I am" to the inscription, so everyone would know this was a false claim by a crazy zealot. But Pilate was adamant.

"What I have written, I have written," he'd uttered through clenched teeth.

No one had dared argue further, and so they had returned to the mount. Caiaphas now questions them again and again, his voice growing louder and angrier. He is consumed with contempt for the Roman procurator.

Does Jesus desire in some way to prove His right to the title they disdain? To rattle the earth beneath their feet or shatter the sky above them? Does He recall the beauty of the throne He once knew as He hangs here from a cross on a hill called Golgotha? Does He consider at all what He would gain by a display of might?

The soldiers on guard duty, aroused by the noisy priests, begin to pace from cross to cross. If only this would go a little quicker. The one in the middle surely can't last much longer, but the other two could stay alive well past sundown.

One of the men, curious after hearing the priests' interchange, examines the words written on each criminal's cross. He mulls over the message that hangs above Christ. *This is Jesus the King of the Jews.*

For now the King wears a crown of thorns. His Majesty's royal robes have been left behind on heaven's gates, bloody stripes and gaping wounds adorning His shoulders instead. And the weight of a sin-sick world lies in the nail-pierced hands that once fashioned it into being. Jesus is dying, but oh how slow the death.

RESPOND

Consider the physical agony Jesus now experiences as He must lift Himself up on His feet in order to exhale. See the suffering on His face as He does so. Know that what you might imagine would most likely fall far short of His abhorrent countenance. "His appearance was marred more than any man and His form more than the sons of men" (Isaiah 52:14 NASB).

Yet He is still the King of kings and Lord of lords. Contemplate the love that keeps Him from asserting His rightful place. Kneel at His feet and worship Him.

PRAYER

My King, I am Your subject even now as Your face, marred beyond recognition, looks down at me. I can still see the compassion in Your weary eyes. I feel the weight of my sin pressing Your shoulders down each time You must drop, Your arms the only support Your body knows. And I bow down. I wash Your feet with my tears, dear and precious Redeemer. What more can I do to ease Your pain?

25 MOCKED

*Age by age the Lord Christ is crucified.
And we too have crowded eagerly to
Calvary and nailed Him to His cross, and
laughed up into His face, and watched
Him die, and gone our way well pleased
and much relieved that we have hustled
Him out of the way—yes, even we.*

—Arthur John Gossip

REFLECT

Step back from the cross for a few minutes and think of Jesus
as the eternal One who once proclaimed:

*Be still, and know that I am God; I will be exalted among
the nations, I will be exalted in the earth.*

—Psalm 46:10 NIV

Worship the exalted Lord, and rest in the quiet of His
presence.

Scripture speaks of Jesus as One rejected by men, but choice
and precious in the sight of God (see 1 Peter 2:4). Have you
ever considered how very precious Jesus was to God the
Father? The love They share has always been and always will
be. The God who exists outside time and space watches men
mock Christ for this brief second of eternity, but to Him the
beauty of His Son burns ever brighter. Let this reality soak in
as you read of this scene today.

READ

> *Those passing by were hurling abuse at Him, wagging their heads and saying, . . . "If You are the Son of God, come down from the cross."*
> —Matthew 27:39–40 NASB

For all practical purposes today is just another day to the inhabitants of Jerusalem. Pilgrims prepare food for the Sabbath. The smell of unleavened bread wafts through the air as children play in the streets. Here and there the conversation among friends and family touches on the Carpenter convicted of treason who now hangs on Golgotha's hill. Some brag of having seen Him do miracles. Others scoff.

The sun beats heavily on those condemned to die. Jesus now sweats profusely, His body rapidly dehydrating. Overcome by chills, He begins to shake from head to toe. Throbbing wrists pound His pulse until it beats like a drum inside His head.

He tries to again lift Himself and breathe, but this time His calves knot up immediately. He falls, wrenching His arms, dislocating one of His shoulders. His eyes fly open and He almost passes out from the torturous pain.

Soon the rumble of conversation around the crosses is interrupted by a raucous group of travelers making their way up the hill. "Aha! There He is. Just look at Him."

Shaking their heads in contempt, they take turns mocking Jesus. "Hey—You up there! You—You who said You could destroy the temple and build it in three days! Save Yourself, then!"

Laughter breaks out among them. Surely this isn't the Man who roared through the temple just yesterday! Where is His pious power now? How disappointing He is to those hoping for some messianic magic. Christ hangs in silence before the taunting crowd.

If You are the Son of God, come down from the cross.

What does Jesus think as they flaunt His impotence in His face? Does the condition of His body make Him oblivious to their jeers? Or does He hear their scorn like a distant chant and long for a touch of kindness from someone, somewhere?

If You are the Son of God, come down from the cross.

Others watch in dismay. Why won't Jesus do something? Is He really going to die? Was every miracle a sham, every word of wisdom a pretense? Flickering flames of hope are slowly extinguished in those who thought it would be different. The would-be Messiah will not come down.

Some turn to leave. There will be no miracles, and the gruesome moment of death on a Roman cross is not worth waiting for. Others continue to sneer, jabbing at Jesus like jesters of the macabre. And the only One who could change things now fights for every agonizing breath. The Son of Man still has much to suffer.

Respond

The physical torture of Jesus has been horrific, but we now move to psychological torture. Consider the atmosphere surrounding the cross as Jesus suffers so. Hear the jeering voices challenging Him to prove Himself. Imagine the spectrum of emotions in the crowd—contempt, disgust, disappointment, hopelessness, anger, insecurity. See their words like arrows piercing the heart of Jesus the Christ. What would it be like to be one of them—ridiculing, rejecting, dismissing Christ's claims to Deity?

Hebrews 2:10 says: "It was fitting for Him, for whom are all things, and through whom are all things, in bringing many sons to glory, to perfect the author of their salvation through sufferings" (NASB). Meditate on the words *It was fitting* as you contemplate all Jesus has endured on Calvary so far. Offer Him your love, adoration, and worship. Write a prayer of thanksgiving based on this verse.

PRAYER

Oh, Lord, how little they understood why You hung there on Calvary. They created You in their own image and when You didn't perform to their expectations, they had no more use for You. They just didn't know, did they? So many times I, too, have demanded You do as I ask, dismissing Your claim on my life when You don't. I stand here with the mockers, passersby who missed completely the eternal significance of Your impending death. And in my selfishness I, too, miss it day after day. Forgive me, dying Savior, for actions that speak louder than words.

26 Scorned

Around the Silent Sufferer surged the brutal slaughter and flung its showers of barbed sarcasm in His holy face. The Prisoner has become the sport of the executioners.

—William E. Biederwolf

Reflect

Let a sense of peace fill your heart as you come to the cross today. Ask God to speak to you afresh, to reveal in some new way the glory of a Savior who lays down His life in love. Ask Him for the privilege of sharing in His suffering.

Psalm 22 is a prophecy of Jesus' time on the cross. It tells us more of Jesus' thoughts as He hung there. Ponder the first part of this psalm, seeking to understand what Jesus felt as you prepare to continue your journey with Him:

My God, my God, why have You forsaken me? Far from my deliverance are the words of my groaning. O my God, I cry by day, but You do not answer; and by night, but I have no rest . . .

But I am a worm and not a man, a reproach of men and despised by the people. All who see me sneer at me; they separate with the lip, they wag the head . . . Be not far from me, for trouble is near; for there is none to help. They open wide their mouth at me, as a ravening and a roaring lion.

—Psalm 22:1–2, 6–7, 11, 13 NASB

READ

> *In the same way the chief priests also, along with the*
> *scribes, were mocking Him among themselves and saying,*
> *"He saved others; He cannot save Himself."*
>
> —Mark 15:31 NASB

As if on cue, the priests and elders take up the ridicule of Christ
that the passersby had begun, now bantering loudly back and
forth.

He saved others; He cannot save Himself.

"Yes—if He is God's chosen One—the Christ, then let's see
Him save Himself!"

Jesus watches but says nothing. Is He envisioning what
would happen if He did save Himself? Can He see demons
binding those below, sealing their slavery to sin for eternity? Or
do His own words—*If you want to save your life, you must*
lose it—echo in His mind?

A mixture of self-righteousness and relief fills the priests as
they see Jesus failing to respond. Surely, now all His foolish followers will understand what a counterfeit this One is who
claimed to be the Christ. Their taunts grow in contempt.

"Look—there's the *King* of Israel!"

Boisterous laughter peppers the air at the absurd idea.
"Sure—He's a *King*, so let Him come down from the cross—
then we'll all believe in Him!"

Nodding in sarcastic agreement, the elders glance at Jesus,
wondering if He'll say or do anything.

What can He say? What words can change the evil in the
hearts of men who glory in His humiliation? What can He do?
Come down from the cross and command them to bow and
give Him His rightful place? How well He understands that if
He did, the price for sin would remain on their heads, a price
none of them can ever hope to pay.

Throughout the ridicule, Caiaphas has stood aloof, enjoying
his moment of triumph. The envy that once ate at his insides

has turned to loathing. He remembers the claims Jesus made only a few hours ago. What a stupid fool.

"He trusts in God. If God loves Him so much, let Him deliver Him right now. After all, He says He is God's own Son!"

Once the chief priest speaks, it seems everyone wants to join in the revelry on Golgotha's hill. Soldiers, inebriated from the wine they have been drinking all morning, revert to their earlier game of pretending Jesus is a king.

A couple of them make grandiose bows before the cross. Another holds up a chalice with the sweet beverage and says, "Come now, O King of the Jews. It is time for You to save Yourself!"

Snickering, they stagger around the cross, toasting each other gaily in the game that provides a break from the monotony of the day.

Like a roar, the scorn at Golgotha reaches the portals of heaven. Myriads of angels mourn, each one yearning to jerk the stakes from Jesus' hands and feet. But the love of God is a mystery into which angels can only long to look. The Savior of the world will not save Himself and let humankind be damned to the hopelessness of hell.

RESPOND

Many people minimize the price Christ paid for sin because they believe since He was God, He had the power to come down if He wanted, or because He knew He would rise again. This is exactly why the price He paid was so great. He could have drawn on His supernatural strength at any moment. He could have forced the issue of His deity, but He chose not to. He chose to embrace the Cross as a man, impotent to changing things.

This is a true mystery. Consider how Jesus had the force of the universe at His disposal, while He chose to endure the pain, the scorn, and the agony of it all. Contemplate the wonder of a love like this. Read or sing the words to the following hymn aloud and write your own prayer in response:

What Wondrous Love Is This?
Alexander Means

What wondrous love is this, O my soul, O my soul!
What wondrous love is this, O my soul!
What wondrous love is this that caused the Lord of bliss
To bear the dreadful curse for my soul, for my soul,
To bear the dreadful curse for my soul?

When I was sinking down, sinking down, sinking down,
When I was sinking down, sinking down,
When I was sinking down beneath God's righteous frown,
Christ laid aside His crown for my soul, for my soul,
Christ laid aside His crown for my soul.

To God and to the Lamb, I will sing, I will sing;
To God and to the Lamb, I will sing.
To God and to the Lamb who is the great "I Am";
While millions join the theme I will sing, I will sing;
While millions join the theme, I will sing.

PRAYER

I wish they understood, my Savior, why You wouldn't save Yourself, but I confess my own perplexity. What kind of love is this? I see Your name sullied by the sins of those You created for glory. I see Your honor disdained by unholiness in hearts You fashioned for Yourself. And still You go to Your death, choosing to endure each moment of torment. I stand here where men scoff and You hang in agony and do not save Yourself and I can only say, my Lord, Your cross confounds me still.

27 TWO RESPONSES

When the true meaning of the crucifixion dawns upon us, then the whole sordid, bloody, painful death shall make us tremble before its glory.

—Ben M. Herbster

REFLECT

Make a conscious effort to stop the activity in your mind as you come before the Lord right now. Slow your thoughts until you can focus on Him. Consider the holy calling He has given you to participate in His sufferings. Ask Him to make this comprehensible to your heart through His Holy Spirit. Read the following words of Thomas à Kempis, reflecting on them and your own life:

> *Jesus hath now many lovers of His heavenly kingdom, but few bearers of His cross. Many He hath that are desirous of consolation, but few of tribulation. Many He findeth that share His table, but few His fasting. All desire to rejoice with Him, few are willing to endure any thing for Him. Many follow Jesus unto the breaking of bread; but few to the drinking of the Cup of His Passion. Many reverence His miracles, few follow the shame of His cross.* (The Imitation of Christ)

Pray for divine revelation as you contemplate the Cross today.

READ

He said to him, "Truly I say to you, today you shall be with Me in Paradise."

—Luke 23:43 NASB

The chorus of mockery surrounding Jesus swells with dissonant notes. Drunken soldiers, pious priests, and sordid onlookers take turns deriding the One who says nothing in return. So intent are they in their scornful quest, none notice the sky starting to swallow the sun at midday.

One of the thieves watches Jesus carefully. For him, hope is slipping away, the terror of death closing in. If this miracle worker beside him has some secret plan, now is the time to execute it. Hoisting himself up, he rails at Jesus.

"Well, are You the Christ or not? Why don't You save Yourself and us, then?" Energy spent, he sags back down, rolling his eyes in disgust.

Jesus turns to him, but he looks away, escaping into his lonely torment.

"How can you say such a thing?" a weak voice challenges from Jesus' other side.

"Don't you fear even God Himself? You are here, condemned to die. You and I—we deserve to be here for the crimes we committed. But this Man has done nothing wrong."

Forcing his words out into the muggy air before his knees collapse, the repentant thief looks to his comrade in crime, but his words fall on deaf ears. For a moment there is silence.

"Jesus."

Jesus slowly turns His head to His right. How odd it must feel to hear His name spoken with such familiarity by this stranger and partner in death.

"Jesus, will You remember me when You come into Your kingdom?"

What an ironic plea offered to the One whose royal reign

must seem no more than a dream in this moment. What might Jesus think as the words break through His private reverie? Surrounded by scoffers, how does it feel to hear this solitary voice of support?

Jesus opens His mouth but cannot speak. Summoning every vestige of strength left in His body, He lifts Himself, and between gasps for air, utters haltingly: "Truly, I . . . say to you, today . . . you shall . . . be with Me . . . in Paradise."

With Me. Does the thought of fellowship refresh Jesus' heart? Can He glimpse for a moment the joy of eternity with those He suffers for even now? Will His final hours before death be more tolerable recalling the penitent thief on His right—the first fruits of atonement?

With Me—never have such beautiful words been spoken. Long ago God's heart broke when He ushered His beloved children out of paradise into a fallen world. But now, in His second word from the cross, Jesus opens the door to the garden of God's presence and lets one sinner in—a fitting reminder that soon the gates will be flung wide to all those who accept His sacrifice for their sins.

The sky grows gray at Golgotha. More of the crowd starts down the slope toward home, fearing bad weather. Staying till the end for a crucifixion is not worth tolerating a Jerusalem thunderstorm.

The soldiers settle down in various stages of drunkenness to await the end, their former games having lost their savor. Only the priests remain the same—proud, haughty, and consumed with righteous contempt for this One who hangs near death.

And angels rejoice at a sinner saved, though their dance is bittersweet.

RESPOND

Two men hung with Jesus on the cross. Both had equal access to Him. But consider the differences:

- — One spoke ridicule—the other spoke truth.
- — One took no responsibility for his sin—the other saw his need.
- — One saw Jesus as a ticket to freedom—the other saw Jesus as a Savior.
- — One hurled abuse—the other pleaded for grace.
- — One faced an eternity of hell—the other entered God's presence that day.

Place yourself there and ask God to show you your own heart. Which thief are you most like? Are there times you can relate to both of them?

Hear Jesus saying these words: *With Me.* What does it mean to be in God's presence—to be *with* Him? Spend some time contemplating this—with Jesus on the cross, with Jesus in death, with Jesus in resurrection, with Jesus in victory . . .

Write a prayer of response.

PRAYER

Dearest dying Lord, deep peace fills my heart when I think of the words You spoke so simply, so eloquently. "With Me" . . . I hear the words and watch You suffer, and I am overcome by the thought. I live in the warmth of Your embrace. I linger in the light of Your kindness. I abide in the hollow of Your heart. Oh, Lord—to be with You is my one great joy, my hope and reason to live. Let me never settle for less than the simplicity of this.

28 ONE LAST ACT OF CARING

> *Whenever anything disagreeable or dis-*
> *pleasing happens to you remember Christ*
> *crucified and be silent.*
>
> —John of the Cross

REFLECT

Prepare your heart to receive from God today and to give back to Him. Spend a few minutes reflecting on how He has blessed your life. Thank Him aloud specifically for these things. Offer these verses as a prayer back to God:

> *My heart is steadfast, O God; I will sing, I will sing praises,*
> *even with my soul. Awake, harp and lyre; I will awaken the*
> *dawn! I will give thanks to you, O LORD, among the peo-*
> *ples, and I will sing praises to You among the nations. For*
> *Your lovingkindness is great above the heavens, and Your*
> *truth reaches to the skies. Be exalted, O God, above the*
> *heavens, and Your glory above all the earth.*
>
> —Psalm 108:1–5 NASB

Consider for a moment the mother of Christ. Recall how as a teenager, an angel came and told her she would give birth to the Savior of the world. After her questions were answered, she responded: "Behold, the bondslave of the Lord; may it be done to me according to your word" (Luke 1:38 NASB). Think of what Mary's life was like as Jesus' mother. Today, walk with her to the cross and see her son being crucified.

READ

Woman, behold, your son!
—John 19:26 NASB

The Jerusalem sky grows darker by the minute, though no clouds can be seen. Those who remain at Golgotha are beginning to feel the weight of the air on their skin. A sense of inexplicable dread settles on the crucifixion crowd. The mockers of a moment ago now find themselves wishing for a speedy end to the day's events.

With eyes squeezed shut, Jesus now pants in short, sharp breaths. His lungs feel as if they are exploding in His chest. How easy it would be to give in, to let Himself be strangled by the air He can't exhale. But it is not yet time.

He pushes down on His feet. Trying to hold Himself up, He spews out breath and gasps for air. There is no relief now to the cramping in His legs, yet He continues to push down. Opening His eyes He scans the hill, taking in face after face until His gaze settles on the small group of women nearby.

He recognizes His two aunts, and Mary of Magdala, whose devotion to Him has been such pure joy in these last months. But all who are watching the eyes of the condemned can see that the woman who captivates His heart is the one who leans against His follower named John. Overcome with emotion, Jesus tries to smile at His mother.

What does He feel when His gaze meets that of the woman who bore Him in her own body? Does His heart break at the sorrow He inflicts on her? Does He remember the times He tried to prepare her for this? How as a child in the temple, He told her He had to be about His Father's business? Or the day He gently rebuked her, saying His family were those who chose to follow Him, and not those related by blood?

Holding Himself up by the force of sheer will, He watches the small group draw closer to the cross. His mother cries quietly as she looks up at her beloved son. It is almost too much to bear.

Woman, behold, your son!

Disturbed by the distress in His voice, Mary reaches out as if longing to caress His face. Racking sobs shake her insides, but she holds her head high. She will not take her eyes from her son's face, though her heart tears in two. John tightens his grip around her shoulder, wishing he could do something, feeling powerless.

"Behold, your mother!" Jesus speaks directly to His brave young disciple. Then without warning, His legs collapse and He drops. John and Mary keep staring, hoping for another word. Jesus tries to encourage them with a nod, but pain contorts His face into an absurd grimace. He closes His eyes.

John gently turns the mother of Christ from the cross, intent on following his Master's final instructions. What more can he do for this One who loved him so in life? Moving back a few feet, the grieving group bow their heads as if in prayer.

Every now and then Mary looks up, hoping for some sign of movement from her child who hovers near death. How she must abhor the burden she bears in these final hours. The shame of illegitimacy brought her firstborn son into the world, and now the shame of crucifixion will take Him from it.

"Be it done unto me according to your word," Mary once said to the angel who illuminated her life with God's wondrous plan. Since Jesus' inglorious birth in a manger she has not wavered in her commitment, but this time the anguish of letting go must be beyond description.

Darkness descends on Golgotha, and demons begin their premature celebration of the Redeemer's defeat. The Son of Man has given up, it seems, death's grip closing in on Him like a vise. But the battle isn't over yet. Though the prince of darkness may wield his victory flag in glee, the Lord of the universe has not yet finished the fight.

RESPOND

Wait quietly upon the Lord as you ponder this scene at Calvary. Consider the intense emotions of Jesus as He says good-bye to His earthly mother. Reflect on her unique pain—both as a mother seeing her son suffer so, and as God's chosen vessel, knowing her task is completed in such a way. Thank God for her presence at the cross, and for that of John—the one disciple who stayed and took no thought for his own life.

Consider Mary's words: "Be it done to me according to your word." As you reflect on the cross of Christ, are you able to offer yourself this willingly? Write a prayer expressing your thoughts in this moment at Calvary.

PRAYER

My precious Lord, give me the courage to pray as Your own mother did, "Be it done to me according to your word." And when I waver, let me remember that though surrender to Your will may cost me a thousand deaths, nothing I suffer can compare with the agony You faced on Golgotha's hill. Oh, that I might join You there, learning of You and loving You. Let me die to gain Your glory and live to bring You pleasure. Let it be, O God, let it be.

29 DARKNESS

Were you there when they crucified
my Lord?
Sometimes it causes me to tremble,
tremble, tremble!

—Traditional Spiritual

REFLECT

Offer yourself completely to the Lord, letting your heart rest in His presence. The time spent contemplating the Cross today will be sobering. To see the scope of what it meant for Christ to drink in all the sin of the world is a serious quest.

Read the following verse a couple of times, putting your name in it:

Christ redeemed us from the curse of the Law, having
become a curse for us— for it is written, "Cursed is every-
one who hangs on a tree."

—Galatians 3:13 NASB

Consider that Christ became a "curse" for you. Write a prayer expressing your heart to God concerning this truth.

READ

From the sixth hour darkness fell upon all the land until
the ninth hour.

—Matthew 27:45 NASB

Only a few hours have passed since the nails were first driven through Jesus' wrists and feet. With each grueling moment it becomes harder to hang on. But He has a cup to drink, and the final dregs of sin's poisonous nectar await Him.

Clenching His teeth, Jesus tightens the throbbing muscles in His arms in order to raise Himself once again. The nails have torn at His wrists, and blood is beginning to ooze from the gaping holes. Before He can catch His breath, He slips and must push Himself up again. After several tries He manages to extend Himself long enough to exhale and replenish His lungs with fresh air.

Then, as if from nowhere, an inky film spreads across the gray sky, turning it completely black. Panic breaks out at Golgotha as people stumble around, bewildered by the strange phenomenon. The soldiers grope their way to the crosses, making sure no one tries to free the condemned. With such a bizarre turn of events, anything seems possible. The crowd huddles in small groups, afraid to move, unable to see even one foot in front of themselves. It is as if the sun has disintegrated.

What goes through the mind of Christ as light leaves the land? Does He remember the days of creation when the earth was formless and void and darkness hovered over it? Does the memory of an eternal expanse undefiled by a people destined to sin call Him back to the Father's side? Does He long to shout, "Let there be light," and end this noontime terror?

Hearts pound fearfully in those left on the mount. The blackness is almost palpable, and it seems the sun will never shine again. Though the air is hot and muggy, a chill engulfs the soldiers and priests. The absence of light at midday fills them with despair.

With every second, Jesus swallows more of humankind's sin. Every disobedient deed, every lustful stare, every evil longing, every act of hatred, every transgression ever perpetrated and every sin yet to be committed, flows like poison into His very soul—drink after drink, until He reaches the dregs of the cup.

Like a disease-infested swamp, the teeming waters of

depravity bring a fatal contamination to the very soul of Christ. He who has never known sin *becomes* the epitome of evil. Darkness oozes in and around Him, its tentacles dragging Him down into the swirling depths of Satan's vile dominion.

And the Light of the world is extinguished for a few hours on a hill called Calvary. Men who love darkness rather than light demand a sign, and God gives them a sky that matches the blackness of their own hearts. No greater horror has ever existed in the history of the world than this day when *darkness fell upon all the land.*

Respond

Try to imagine the blackness that descended on Calvary. Contemplate the physical impact of it first. Then, reflect on a world where Light—every vestige of God's presence—is gone, and only the darkness of evil remains. Place yourself in the midst of the most vile circumstances you can imagine where sin reigns and no good exists—no kindness, love, joy, compassion, trust, gentleness, or peace.

The atmosphere is terrifying—hatred, bitterness, lust, greed, rage, lying, cheating, murder, rape, gossip, backbiting, hopelessness so severe people gnash their teeth and rail at one another. This is what reigns on Calvary when Jesus drinks in the sin of the world and becomes a curse for you and for me. Give yourself enough time to feel this. Envision your own sins—yesterday's, today's, and tomorrow's in the cup Jesus drank there.

When you think you have even a tiny grasp of the price Jesus paid for you in those three hours of darkness, read these verses: "He rescued us from the domain of darkness, and transferred us to the kingdom of His beloved Son, in whom we have redemption, the forgiveness of sins" (Colossians 1:13–14 NASB).

Feel the relief of this truth, rejoice in the wonder of it, and worship your Redeemer with a heart of pure and overwhelming gratitude.

PRAYER

Oh, my God, the darkness frightens me even now. My hands shake and I scream for light. I cannot live except You illumine my sinful soul. How can You drink this cup? I cannot comprehend it, but this I know—had You stopped short and refused even one final drop, I would dwell forever in the hopelessness of eternity's dark night. Oh, my God, I fall on my knees.

DEATH

Who killed Jesus? Like a loaded gun, this question was bandied about in anticipation of the movie *The Passion of the Christ*. From pinstriped preachers to politically correct pundits, experts took aim at the age-old question.

Isaiah tells us Jesus was "smitten of God" and, in fact, that "the LORD was pleased to crush Him" (Isaiah 53:4, 10 NASB). How can this be? How could God smite His own Son, and take pleasure in doing so? To grasp this, we must survey the sweeping scope of the gospel story, one that began before the foundation of the world.

In the beginning there was only God, the eternal Other so grand and glorious that He took supreme delight in displaying and exalting His own beauty. In need of nothing, He created a world, and made man in His image that we might know the joy of experiencing and extolling His worth. But instead, we scorned Him, seeking to satisfy our souls with things like sex and success and cars and clothes and careers and a multitude of other, lesser loves.

What shall a God, who loves His glory *and* the sinners who disdain it, do? His holiness demands He exact a price commensurate with both the magnitude of the offense and His extravagant worth. And so, in a mystery humankind will never completely understand or fully appreciate, Almighty God crushes His own Son, the only feasible propitiation.

The joy set before Jesus as He endured the Cross, and His Father's pleasure in putting Him to death, was the vindication of His honor while saving the sinners He loved, the very ones who had sullied that honor. May the wonder of this settle upon us as we journey with Jesus these final moments.

30 FORSAKEN

> *There is something infinitely profounder*
> *than pathos in the death of Jesus; there is a*
> *mystery we cannot begin to touch.*
>
> —Oswald Chambers

REFLECT

Breathe deeply as you settle your heart before God. Release the distractions of your day, concentrating on the presence of Christ in and around you through His Spirit. Do this until you feel ready to contemplate what God has for you today.

Quietly read Amos 8:9–10, a prophecy of the darkness at Golgotha:

> *"It will come about in that day," declares the Lord GOD,*
> *"that I will make the sun go down at noon and make the*
> *earth dark in broad daylight. Then I will turn your festi-*
> *vals into mourning and all your songs into lamentation;*
> *and I will bring sackcloth on everyone's loins and bald-*
> *ness on every head. And I will make it like a time of*
> *mourning for an only son, and the end of it will be like a*
> *bitter day."* (NASB)

Imagine the atmosphere God describes. See rejoicing turning to mourning, and happy songs turning to loud, mournful laments at the gloom of a world without Light. Ask God to reveal the reality of this so that you may mourn for His only Son as you come to the cross today.

READ

> *About the ninth hour Jesus cried out with a loud voice,*
> *saying, "Eli, Eli, lama sabachthani?" that is, "My God,*
> *My God, why have You forsaken Me?"*
>
> —Matthew 27:46 NASB

The darkness on Golgotha is so thick now that no one dares move. The air reeks of hopelessness. Sweeping depression descends on everyone who attends the crucifixion of Jesus of Nazareth. Some begin to shake uncontrollably; others weep in silent despair. Priests clutch their phylacteries like good luck charms, but relief doesn't come.

Jesus writhes in agony as He drinks the final drops from sin's vile cup. His back is a mass of infection, pus oozing from raw sores. His grotesque face contorts in the blackness at midday. Thankfully no one can see His repugnant form. When finally He swallows the last of the bitter potion, His body explodes in convulsions of racking pain.

Flinging Himself up with inhuman strength, He screams: "My God, My God, why have You forsaken Me?"

What rips such a plea from the bowels of the crucified One? Is hope completely obscured by the darkness of the sin He carries? Is the onslaught of demonic forces threatening His determination to endure till the end?

The priests are startled at first, then find themselves strangely discomforted at this show of weakness. Sobered soldiers fight their own internal demons. Abject woe wrenches the hearts of the women who hear their beloved Rabbi scream in the distance.

"My God, My God, why have You forsaken Me?" Jesus cries out, but there is no answer. What inner turmoil must plague the Son at this severing of His triune soul? From Gethsemane till now, God the Father has refused to intervene. What kind of wretchedness wields its way into His Son's heart at such rejection? Does sovereign silence sabotage His struggle to obey for even an instant?

With great force Jesus is plunged back down, paralyzing the muscles in His arms. Then, for no apparent reason, the sky begins to lighten. Those nearby look up to examine the face of the One who has screamed in such distress. How can one explain what they see? For though racked with pain and battered beyond belief, something strange emanates from His eyes. It almost seems a look of relief.

And God the Father weeps great sobs, shaking the heavens with His grief. How hard it has been to restrain Himself while watching His Son endure such agony. How He has longed to intervene—to subdue the suffering for even a moment. What torment He has known in every drop of sin His Son has drunk.

But His righteousness requires such a reckoning, and the plan put into place so long ago must be carried out to the bitter end. Never has the world known a moment such as this, when mercy triumphs over judgment and love restrains the Almighty, silencing His voice. The price is paid—by the Son who dies and the Father who could save Him but declines on behalf of a lost and dying world.

RESPOND

It is beyond our human comprehension to fathom what happened when Christ took on the sins of the world. Yet, as worshipers, we must try. Place yourself in that state of darkness once again, and listen to Jesus cry from the cross: "My God, My God, why have You forsaken Me?" What would it be like to know your only parent will not help you in your time of greatest need?

In reality, God did not turn His back on Jesus, but chose again and again to not intervene, that the price of sin might be paid in full. As you hear Jesus cry out, consider both His pain and the Father's. Consider the agony of watching your only child suffer, knowing you must not reach out to help.

Read the following verses and rejoice that He is your source of eternal salvation.

In the days of His flesh, He offered up both prayers and supplications with loud crying and tears to the One able to save Him from death, and He was heard because of His piety. Although He was a Son, He learned obedience from the things which He suffered. And having been made perfect, He became to all those who obey Him the source of eternal salvation.

—Hebrews 5:7–9 NASB

Spend some time in worship for all that has been done to purchase you from sin's grip. Write a prayer based on these verses.

PRAYER

Father God, how rarely have I thought of Your pain in watching Your Son die as He did. I dismiss it with tenets of theology and lofty explanations. But You were there. You did not leave—that perhaps would have been easier. You stayed . . . and You watched . . . and You wept . . . and You did nothing. You refused to act—truly I am unworthy of such love. I rest in my unworthiness and ponder the mercy flowing down for one such as me.

31 Thirsty

How do you approach the thirst of Jesus?
Only one secret—the closer you come to
Jesus, the better you will know His thirst.
Jesus thirsts even now, in your heart and in
the poor—He knows your weakness, He
wants only your love, wants only the
chance to love you.

—Mother Teresa

Reflect

Come to the oasis of God's refreshing presence as you seek
Him today. Spend a few minutes thanking Him for the living
water, which is always available for you to drink. Consider
what it means to be truly thirsty and unable to quench your
thirst.

Another prophecy of the Crucifixion is found in Psalm 69.
Read the following verses and contemplate the emotions of
Christ as He hangs in the final moments on Golgotha:

Save me, O God, for the waters have threatened my life.
I have sunk in deep mire, and there is no foothold; I have
come into deep waters, and a flood overflows me. I am
weary with my crying; my throat is parched; my eyes fail
while I wait for my God.

Those who hate me without a cause are more than the
hairs of my head; those who would destroy me are pow-
erful, being wrongfully my enemies; what I did not steal,
I then have to restore . . .

*Reproach has broken my heart and I am so sick. And
I looked for sympathy, but there was none, and for com-
forters, but I found none. They also gave me gall for my
food and for my thirst they gave me vinegar to drink.*
—Psalm 69:1–4, 20–21 NASB

Read the verses again, ponder them, and ask God to reveal
the deeper truths in Jesus' cry: "I am thirsty."

READ

*After this, Jesus, knowing that all things had already been
accomplished, to fulfill the Scripture, said, "I am thirsty."*
—John 19:28 NASB

The faint light spreading across Golgotha stirs groups of
onlookers who have been frozen in fear. Most hurry home,
anxious to leave behind an overpowering sense of dread and
despair. The four soldiers, superstitious about the receding
darkness, stand apprehensively near the crosses. Soon, stilted
conversations begin as different ones offer their opinions on
the black sky and the forlorn cry from Jesus' lips.

One of the priests surmises: "Clearly, He is calling for
Elijah!" Nervous snickers ensue as they discuss the absurdity
of such a plea.

The physical pain for Jesus drones on, a persistent vibration
in every cell of His failing body. Yet, the agony on His face is different now. In the eye of suffering's terrible storm, it almost
seems He has found a place of rest. He looks out over Jerusalem,
recalling His days and nights of obedience to His Father. Now,
in this moment, a sense of completion settles in His soul. He has
done what He came to do.

Death is near. Jesus pants faster, gasping for air with each
try. His lungs ache from the stress, and His throat burns with
each breath. His heart must work harder and harder to pump
blood throughout His body. Dehydrated and no longer able to

swallow, He manages to push Himself up just enough to mouth the words *I am thirsty*.

What goes through His mind as He speaks? Is it physical thirst that compels Him to cry out so? Or do the words tell a deeper story? Does He thirst on behalf of a lost and dying world desperate for a taste of the living water only He can give? Is He gently reminding those who will follow Him that in quenching the thirst of humanity, they quench His own thirst? That a cup of water given to the least of these will now and forever be a cup of water for Him?

One of the soldiers grabs a reed from a hyssop plant, putting a sponge on its tip. He dips it in his own cup of cheap wine and holds it to Jesus' lips. The priests and elders, put off at the act of kindness, taunt Him once again.

"Ha—leave Him alone and see if Elijah will come and take Him down!"

"Yes—let us see if Elijah will come and save Him now!"

The laughter resumes, though it lacks the force of their earlier sarcasm. The vinegary wine, burning Jesus' cracked lips and parched tongue, drips down His face. The sun grows brighter, beating down on His matted head while His body shivers uncontrollably.

Within the city the celebration of Passover comes slowly to an end. Families have broken bread and offered their finest lambs in sacrifice and homage to Yahweh. And on the hill outside the city gates, the Lamb of God stands at the very threshold of death, having finally and fully offered Himself as the ultimate sacrifice for a world bound by sin.

RESPOND

Let yourself feel a small sense of the peace that Christ is experiencing on a spiritual level at nearing completion of the work on the cross. Yet, know that the physical pain continues. Imagine His thirst, having had nothing to eat or drink for hours, hanging in the hot sun, tongue swollen and lips cracked open and dry. Then consider His longing to give living water to all who want to drink. Hear Him say, "I am thirsty." Contemplate His voice and these two words for a while. What do the words mean to you?

Read Psalm 22:14–15, reflecting on Jesus' state of mind: "I am poured out like water, and all my bones are out of joint; my heart is like wax; it is melted within me. My strength is dried up like a potsherd, and my tongue cleaves to my jaws; and You lay me in the dust of death" (NASB).

How will you respond to His thirst? What difference will it make in your own life? Write a prayer of response to Him as He calls to you personally, "I am thirsty."

PRAYER

Oh, Jesus, how I long to quench Your thirst. I see You there, and I want to run with a cool glass of water from a fresh spring. For this is what You did for me when my soul dwelled in a dry and thirsty land. You came rushing in, O River of Life, and now from my innermost being flow forth springs of living water. I will quench Your thirst, dearest Savior. To a lost and dying world, I will offer a cup in Your name.

32 IT IS FINISHED

Blessed Redeemer, precious Redeemer,
seems now I see Him on Calvary's tree.
—Avis B. Christiansen

REFLECT

Spend some time as you begin today just being silent, stilling all the sounds within and without. Breathe in His great love and breathe out your own self-centeredness. Breathe in His commitment to you, and breathe out your own commitments to things with no eternal value. Ask God to purify your heart.

Read or sing the words to the following hymn, contemplating the depth of each phrase:

Beneath the Cross of Jesus
Elizabeth Cecelia Clephane

Beneath the cross of Jesus I fain would take my stand—
The shadow of a mighty Rock within a weary land;
A home within the wilderness, a rest upon the way,
From the burning of the noontide heat, and the burden of
*   the day.*

Upon that cross of Jesus mine eye at times can see
The very dying form of One who suffered there for me;
And from my smitten heart with tears two wonders I
*   confess—*
The wonders of redeeming love and my unworthiness.
I take, O cross, thy shadow for my abiding place;

I ask no other sunshine than the sunshine of His face;
Content to let the world go by, to know no gain nor loss,
My sinful self my only shame, my glory all the cross.

READ

> *When Jesus had received the sour wine, He said, "It is*
> *finished!"*
>
> —John 19:30 NASB

Every eye in the small crowd left at the cross is on Jesus. Death is imminent, and many are curious to see how He will go. Passersby who have stayed till the end still hope to get their money's worth. Perhaps the would-be king will perform some last-minute miracle. The priests, anxious for Him to breathe His final breath, keep a detached vigil at His feet.

The thieves on either side of Christ have begun to thrash about, groaning loudly. But unlike most victims of crucifixion, Jesus does not fight the throes of death. Hanging there so still, it appears that perhaps He has passed on.

But then He moves. Gingerly He presses His bloody feet into the stipe once again. Lifting only a couple of inches, His eyes scan the vast horizon, then settle on those below. Forcing the air from His lungs, He sucks in as much breath as He can. Then, as if to announce to all that His time has come, Jesus cries out haltingly: "It . . . is . . . finished!"

What images flash across His memory as He utters these final words to humankind? Does His short span on earth now spin like a panorama of events through His mind? Visions of Peter throwing out his nets for the catch of a lifetime, then leaving it all behind to follow Him? Parents bringing their children to sit on His lap and be blessed? Adulterers, prostitutes, liars, and thieves coming to Him for restoration? Religious leaders hungry for spiritual truth, seeking Him out in the middle of the night? The blind seeing, the lame leaping, the demonized delivered and even dead men walking?

Does He recall the dozens of prophecies concerning Him, rejoicing that every one is finally fulfilled? Can He hear His Father proclaiming once again, "This is My beloved Son, in whom I am well-pleased"?

It is finished. He speaks words replete with symbolism, and some standing here ponder the message. He could be saying so many things: It is accomplished . . . the debt is discharged . . . the plan has been executed . . . the task is complete. Even the soldiers stop and stare, turning the three words over in their minds.

Satan hears and gloats in tawdry triumph. He calls for the festivities to begin, believing he has won after all. Demons dance and toast each other, drinking to their own degradation. The Son of God will die like everyone else.

It is finished. Jesus wraps His dying words in an eternity of truth. By one man sin entered the world, bringing the condemnation of death to all. And now by one Man the gift of eternal life can be freely bestowed upon all those who believe.

It is finished. In His final seconds, as Jesus considers the world into which He came, perhaps one thought prevails. Soon He will have a people for His own possession, an inheritance to present to His Father, that they might see His beauty and live in the wonder of triune love, tasting at last the eternal joy for which humankind was made.

This has cost Him dearly, and many will never understand how much. But from the foundation of the world, the heart of the infinite I AM has waited for this moment when Jesus the Christ, dying a despicable death on a Roman cross, can proclaim, "It is finished."

RESPOND

Stop for a moment, breathing in the sense of wonder that filled Christ as He saw His completed work. Consider all the days and nights that have led up to this—especially the last several hours. Contemplate the suffering that He endured. Hear Him speak to you, calling you by name: "It is finished. Your sins are forgiven, washed white as snow. Your debt is paid. You are free. I have redeemed you not with silver or gold, but with My precious blood. You are bought with this painful price. Now you will see My glory. I delight to give you My love. It is finished."

Romans 8:31–32 says: "What then shall we say to these things? If God is for us, who is against us? He who did not spare His own Son, but delivered Him over for us all, how will He not also with Him freely give us all things?" (NASB). Think of these words in light of your understanding of Christ's death on the cross. What new meaning do they have? Offer a prayer of worship and thanksgiving based on these verses.

PRAYER

O my Father, You are truly for me . . . for me. What in the world can I say to such a thought? You spared nothing—not even Your own precious Son—that I might know You and live in the circle of Your love for eternity. How can I ever doubt You? How can I ever question Your plans for me? You, who freely give me all things, have given me Yourself. What more could I ever need to satisfy this soul?

33   THE END

> *As you gaze upon the cross, and long for*
> *conformity to him, be not weary or fearful*
> *because you cannot express in words what*
> *you seek. Ask him to plant the cross in*
> *your heart. Believe in him, the crucified*
> *and now living one, to dwell within you,*
> *and breathe his own mind there.*
>
> —Andrew Murray

REFLECT

There are mysteries we will never fully understand concerning the death of Jesus on the cross. Ask God today to open your spiritual eyes to something new concerning His sacrifice. Place your heart at the foot of His cross, content to spend time meditating, reflecting, and rejoicing at what has happened. Remember Jesus' words to Pilate that the power to take His life comes only from God (see John 19:11). Thank Him for making the choice even to the very end that enables your own redemption.

READ

> *Jesus, crying out with a loud voice, said, "Father, into*
> *Your hands I commit My spirit."*
>
> —Luke 23:46 NASB

Six hours have passed since the Crucifixion began. The soldiers, sensitive to every nuance of death on a cross, know the end is nigh for the peculiar criminal in the middle. He is going quickly now, but for those who love Him, every minute must seem an endless marathon of misery.

His back resembles raw meat. His face is ghastly, bruised and mangled, with rivulets of dried blood from the crown of thorns etched like furrows upon it. Lacerated from the scourging, the wounds have bred ugly abscesses in the hours He has repeatedly rubbed against the stipe. His whole body shakes in the tremors of one succumbing to infection.

Watching Him now, it is as if time is suspended on Calvary. Almost in slow motion, He lifts Himself. Then with a force that shocks even the most disinterested bystanders, He screams: "Father, into Your hands I commit My spirit!"

With this, He exhales all the air left in His lungs. His body collapses and in one final act of humility, Jesus the Christ bows His head, giving up His Spirit. He is gone, completing the cycle for which all of creation has longed since Adam first sinned in the Garden of Eden. From the Father He came into the world, and now to the Father He returns.

This final exclamation is a mystery to all. There is no sound of defeat; these certainly are not words of despair. This is the cry of a conqueror and the voice of victory. No one knows quite what to make of it.

All of antiquity has led up to this, and all history will point back to it. To many it will seem a foolish thing that One claiming to be God's Son should die in such a way. But to those who will be washed in the healing streams of the blood shed on Golgotha's hill, the war cry Jesus bellows as He embraces death—*Father, into Your hands I commit My spirit*—is the very power of God for salvation.

RESPOND

Can you imagine what it must have felt like to hear Jesus shout these final words? Consider the strength He felt, the complete sense of control He had over His own destiny. Even at the conclusion of such terrible suffering, even while His body shrieks with pain, He cries out with strength and power. Consider the joy He must have felt as He offered His Spirit back to the Father from whom He had come. What an incredible reunion They must have had. Rejoice with the living God at this moment of victory.

Read these verses quietly:

> *When you were dead in your transgressions and the uncircumcision of your flesh, He made you alive together with Him, having forgiven us all our transgressions, having canceled out the certificate of debt consisting of decrees against us, which was hostile to us; and He has taken it out of the way, having nailed it to the cross.*
> —Colossians 2:13–14 NASB

Read them again aloud, placing your name in the passage, turning it into a prayer of praise (e.g., *Oh, God, when I was dead in my vile sin, You made me alive together with You . . .*). Write it out and commit to rejoicing throughout this day at the truth of it.

PRAYER

Oh, God, I hear Your victory cry and I want to shout too. My heart has wept with You, and now I rejoice in Your joy at going to Your Father. I see You leaving that cross, and there stained with Your life's blood are my own sins—a certificate of debt I could never pay—nailed to the wood with the spikes that once held You there. But You are gone; You have paid it all, and I wonder how I can ever express my praise.

34   THE EARTH RESPONDS

*But as we gaze, it is not pity that we feel,
but a profound reverence, for there on
Calvary is the great turning point in the
course of human affairs.*

—Hughell Fosbroke

REFLECT

Come to the Lord today with simple gratitude for His great love.
Rest in Him for a few minutes, offering words of adoration.

Consider the turning point in history that Jesus' death
brought about. Besides the spiritual impact, think of how our
world revolves around the event—our calendar being based on
it. Muse for a few minutes on the concept that for nearly two
thousand years, the gospel of Jesus Christ has spread continu-
ously, changing lives of people from every race and nation as it
now spans the entire globe. Ask God to plant a sense of awe
about this within you, as you reflect on the first minutes after
His death.

READ

The veil of the temple was torn in two from top to bottom.
—Mark 15:38 NASB

The very bowels of the earth reverberate at the death of Jesus
of Nazareth on a hill outside Jerusalem. Those attending the
Crucifixion notice it first—a rumbling beneath their feet. Soon

the ground begins to roll in ripple after ripple, causing many to lose their balance.

Then without warning the hillside ruptures, creating zigzag crevices large enough to swallow one whole. Giant boulders simply disappear from view, and confusion runs rampant on Golgotha and throughout the city. Hebrew families, familiar with ancestral stories of God's judgment through acts of nature, wonder what great sin has taken place.

It is the time of the evening sacrifice, and several priests have made their way to the temple to burn incense. They, too, feel the ground quaking, and as they clutch tables to keep from falling, something incomprehensible occurs. With a sound like the roar of the sea, the heavy curtain separating them from the holy of holies begins to come apart at the top. The fine linen shimmers and shakes, its shades of purple, violet, and scarlet blending together.

Frozen, the priests watch as the veil, which normally takes the strength of three hundred to handle every year on the Day of Atonement, tears in two from top to bottom. It is an awesome and frightening sight to behold. In splendorous display, the ark of the covenant stands gleaming before their very eyes. Stunned, the priests begin to back away.

What must they feel as they encounter this sacred object? Does the cloud of God's presence hover over the mercy seat as it did in Moses' day? Do they fall down in wonder or cower in fear before the God whose law demands that only one man enter this place, and only once a year? Will some of these priests soon put their faith in Jesus the Messiah as a result of what they've seen here?

The earth continues to convulse, and what happens next defies the wildest imagination. Boulders that once sealed tombs begin to break apart, and through the rubble bodies that have long been dead arise. No one will ever know how many are given this resurrection gift, but in the coming week, many of these miracle men and women will shock family and friends as they appear throughout Jerusalem.

No one can deny that something of cataclysmic significance

is taking place in this moment of crucifixion. The earth shakes, rocks shatter, and the dead come to life. The veil of the temple tears in two, admitting common priests into the holy of holies where God's presence resides and the blood of bulls is sprinkled annually to atone for sin. Almighty God acknowledges the death of His Son in a dramatic way.

And yet all these things are merely a shadow of the beauty and power displayed in the heavenlies when the veil of Jesus' flesh was rent, sprinkling His blood across the altar of history. For this sacrificial Lamb atones for sins, not once a year, but once and for all, leading the way for humankind to live forever in the wonder of God's holy presence.

RESPOND

Think about the freedom that you have to enjoy God's presence day in and day out, knowing that His Spirit will never leave you. Leviticus details God's plan for a Day of Atonement for the Israelites (see chapter 16). In it, only one person was allowed in the place where God's presence resided, and then only once per year to offer sacrifices for the sins of all. If anyone disobeyed, they would die.

In light of that, ponder the truths in the following passage:

> *Every priest stands daily ministering and offering time after time the same sacrifices, which can never take away sins; but He, having offered one sacrifice for sins for all time, sat down at the right hand of God . . . Therefore, brethren, since we have confidence to enter the holy place by the blood of Jesus, by a new and living way which He inaugurated for us through the veil, that is, His flesh, and since we have a great priest over the house of God, let us draw near with a sincere heart in full assurance of faith, having our hearts sprinkled clean from an evil conscience and our bodies washed with pure water.*
> —Hebrews 10:11–12, 19–22 NASB

Thank Jesus Christ for everything this passage tells you about your relationship with Him and salvation through Him. Write a list and offer it up as a sacrifice of praise to the Author of your own salvation.

PRAYER

Jesus, I remember the first time I saw, really saw the beauty of Your Being. Holiness and humility, justice and mercy, righteousness and grace—all that You are my soul could finally glimpse because You suffered and died on Calvary. You led the way; You rent forever the veil between us and I followed You in. I ran through Your broken body and spilled blood into the holy of holies where You shone the light of Your glory . . . how great my joy.

35 REACTIONS

> *As you sit and gaze, it will be born in you*
> *that only a crucified Savior could meet*
> *your need.*
>
> —William Sangster

REFLECT

Wait before God today, rejoicing that He is faithful to meet you here regardless of what you have done or what you feel. The truth that He never leaves or forsakes you is a foundation you can rest in right now.

Read the following verses aloud, personalizing them as a song of praise to the living God. Rejoice that you are able to proclaim the tidings of His salvation because of His work on the cross:

> *Sing to the LORD a new song; sing to the LORD, all the*
> *earth. Sing to the LORD, bless His name; proclaim good*
> *tidings of His salvation from day to day. Tell of His glory*
> *among the nations, His wonderful deeds among all the*
> *peoples.*
>
> —Psalm 96:1–3 NASB

READ

> *When the centurion, who was standing right in front of*
> *Him, saw the way He breathed His last, he said, "Truly*
> *this man was the Son of God!"*
>
> —Mark 15:39 NASB

Though the earth has begun to settle down, unrest plagues Calvary's crucifixion crowd. The few small groups of people who remain long to run, to escape the terror of what they've just experienced. They do not know that what happened here has affected the entire universe.

The soldiers cautiously approach the dead criminal. Images from the past six hours assail them, filling their minds with apprehension. The centurion in charge lifts his hands as if beseeching the heavens, his eyes glued to the face of Christ. Jesus' countenance is a peaceful one, His bruises and cuts seeming to have faded with His passing.

How different this death is from all the others the soldiers have witnessed. Absorbed in thought, they ponder the paradox that One brutally nailed to a cross could determine His own destiny, even to His last breath. A hushed stillness surrounds the small circle of military men, and in awe the centurion whispers: "Truly this man was the Son of God."

Another group stands in quiet reverence before the cross. There is Mary of Magdala, whom Jesus once set free from the torment of seven demons. Her shell-shocked eyes stare silently at the body of Christ in death. There are His aunts, and other women who had left everything to follow Him, gladly supporting Jesus and the disciples out of their own resources. Exhausted, they hold one another in silent grief, weeping no longer.

And there is His mother, Mary. On her knees, she rocks back and forth with face in hands, not making a sound. John stands at her side, fighting the flood of emotion within.

Some religious men, frightened by the turn of events, begin to beat at their breasts, pleading for God to have mercy on their souls. Others simply shake their heads in disbelief. The last of the crowd begins to break up, and a subdued procession winds its way down Golgotha's hill, back to the business of life.

Most are filled with relief that the ordeal is over. Many are numb, confused, and emotionally spent. But in the moments after the death of Jesus on Calvary's cross, one soldier encounters the Savior. *Truly this man was the Son of God.* In childlike trust, he speaks words of faith, and like millions who will join him in the centuries to come, nothing will ever be the same.

RESPOND

Think of what the centurion experienced when he realized who Jesus was. Contemplate the sense of awe that filled him, and the faith he demonstrated when he spoke aloud what he saw.

Do you remember when you first discovered the truth about Jesus Christ? Whether it was as a child through a Sunday school book, as a teenager, or as an adult, take the time to reminisce those moments. Relive in your heart the wonder and fresh awareness that Jesus died for you. Embrace anew the joy of your salvation.

Write a prayer of gratitude for your personal salvation.

PRAYER

Dearest Savior, truly You are the Son of God. I, too, cannot look at You in death without wonder. How You suffered . . . Will I ever be able to think of Your sacrifice without feeling the freshness of Your wounds, or reliving the grief of Your sorrow? Holy One, righteous in all Your ways, I adore You, but You deserve so much more. Give me grace, Lord, to live for Your pleasure, to fight for Your honor, and magnify Your worth for a world that has yet to believe.

36 WATER AND BLOOD

> *Stand at the foot of the cross, and count*
> *the purple drops by which you have been*
> *cleansed; see the thorn-crown; mark His*
> *scourged shoulders, still gushing with*
> *encrimsoned rills . . . And if you do not lie*
> *prostrate on the ground before that cross,*
> *you have never seen it.*
>
> —Charles Haddon Spurgeon

REFLECT

As you come before the Lord today, consider what it must have been like to have been a Hebrew celebrating Passover. For centuries, fathers have used this event to pass down to their children the story of how Jehovah spared them from death in Egypt by having them mark their doorposts with the blood of a pure, unblemished lamb (see Exodus 12).

Ephesians 1:7–8 says:

In Him we have redemption through His blood, the forgiveness of our trespasses, according to the riches of His grace which He lavished on us. (NASB)

Reflect on the fact that Jesus' blood is a sign over you, a gift of His lavish grace, that you may escape terrible judgment and punishment and embrace new life. Jesus is our Passover Lamb. Muse on this for a few moments.

Now, very slowly, read the following passage:

If you address as Father the One who impartially judges according to each one's work, conduct yourselves in fear during the time of your stay on earth; knowing that you were not redeemed with perishable things like silver or gold from your futile way of life inherited from your fore-fathers, but with precious blood, as of a lamb unblemished and spotless, the blood of Christ.

—1 Peter 1:17–19 NASB

Read it again, offering specific words of thanksgiving for everything it tells you about you and your relationship to Christ.

READ

He who has seen has testified, and his testimony is true; and he knows that he is telling the truth, so that you also may believe.

—John 19:35 NASB

As evening draws near, only the soldiers and a handful of priests remain on Golgotha. The two thieves continue to groan occasionally, rising up as they spew out each agonizing breath. Jesus seems shrouded in death, yet no one can be absolutely sure. With the Sabbath approaching, Caiaphas worries that they won't all die before sundown.

Sacred law is clear on this: No criminal is to hang from a tree overnight. The thousands of pilgrims who have come to Jerusalem for Passover will certainly question his own authority if these bodies are left to hang.

Disturbed, he sends one of the elders with an urgent message to Pilate, requesting an order for the bones of the dying men to be broken. Once this is done and they can no longer lift themselves up to exhale, they will suffocate in a matter of minutes. As he waits for an answer, the chief priest paces impatiently, wanting to be done with the whole sordid saga. Finally, a runner approaches with the order bearing Pilate's seal.

The centurion reads it and picking up a large iron bar, motions to one of the soldiers to begin. The soldier nods and moves to the thief on the right, striking a vicious blow just below the knees. The criminal cries out, then collapses. The bar is handed off to another soldier, who does the same to the thief on the left.

The third soldier takes the bar and approaches Jesus, but just as he lifts it up, the centurion calls out for him to wait. The three soldiers step back with questioning looks. The centurion knows that Pilate will want proof of death, but for some inexplicable reason feels compelled to keep them from breaking this One's bones. Clearly Jesus is dead, and has been for a while. Why bother?

Torn, he finally pulls out his lance and faces Jesus, quickly plunging it into His heart. A stream of liquid shoots forth, spraying the air and splattering him. Dumbfounded, he stares at the strange mixture of thick red blood and clear liquid spewing from Jesus' side.

The soldiers exchange curious glances. What an odd crucifixion this has been. Nothing about this prisoner's behavior has seemed normal. Now in His death He bleeds blood and water, a sight they've never seen in all the hundreds of executions they've witnessed.

Night is beginning to fall and the last of the priests and elders, content that Jesus is dead, hurry home before the sun sets in the west. The soldiers begin to clean up the area around the crosses where debris from the day is scattered.

As news of the mysterious phenomenon of blood and water spreads throughout Jerusalem, some pause to consider what it might mean. There are those who say Jesus died of a broken heart, the blood-and-water mix pure proof. It reminds others of how He had claimed to be Living Water, and His promise that rivers would flow out of their innermost beings as well, if only they would believe. Naysayers mock the soldiers' story, certain such a thing could never have happened.

One day this scene will flash in front of every person who

has ever walked this earth. Every eye will gaze at Jesus' pierced side, and they will mourn as if they have lost their only son, for all of humankind has played a part in His gruesome death. But today on a hill outside Jerusalem, only a few stragglers witness the amazing enigma of blood and water flowing like a fountain from the side of the Carpenter from Nazareth.

RESPOND

Spend some time gazing at Jesus in death on Calvary. Allow your mind to recall various scenes from this place—the words He spoke, the compassion He showed, the gentleness He demonstrated, and the choice He continued to make to offer Himself till the very end. As you contemplate these things, worship Him.

Read the following prophecies:

I will pour out on the house of David and on the inhabitants of Jerusalem, the Spirit of grace and of supplication, so that they will look on Me whom they have pierced; and they will mourn for Him, as one mourns for an only son, and they will weep bitterly over Him like the bitter weeping over a firstborn.

—Zechariah 12:10 NASB

Behold, He is coming with the clouds, and every eye will see Him, even those who pierced Him; and all the tribes of the earth will mourn over Him. So it is to be. Amen.

—Revelation 1:7 NASB

Look on the One whom you, too, have pierced with your own sin. Feel a sense of mourning at your part in His death, but also rejoice that He will come again in glory as the King of kings, and all will understand the price He paid. Offer words of praise for this reality. Write a prayer of thanksgiving.

PRAYER

Jesus, even now, I look at You—at Your side as it flows with water and blood. It is a fountain in which I cannot plunge deep enough, dearest Savior. I feel Your heart break for me, and I know that I, too, have pierced You with my indifference, my rebellious clutch at control, and my callous disregard for the price You paid to change all this. I see in Your blood the great sacrifice and I take comfort in the cleansing streams that ever flow from Your side. Wash me here, Lord, and I will be whiter than snow.

37   TAKEN DOWN

For in the cross of Christ, as in a splendid theater, the incomparable goodness of God is set before the whole world. The glory of God shines, indeed, in all creatures on high and below, but never more brightly than in the cross.

—Calvin's St. John

REFLECT

We have walked the entire journey with Christ to the cross, and soon His body will be taken down. What joy we can embrace as we comprehend His great achievement on Calvary. Quiet your heart before God, and read (or sing) slowly the words to the following old hymn. Let the words set your heart toward your blessed Redeemer.

When I Survey the Wondrous Cross
Isaac Watts

When I survey the wondrous cross
On which the Prince of glory died,
My richest gain I count but loss,
And pour contempt on all my pride.

Forbid it, Lord, that I should boast,
Save in the death of Christ, my God;
All the vain things that charm me most—
I sacrifice them to His blood.

See, from His head, His hands, His feet,
Sorrow and love flow mingled down;
Did e'er such love and sorrow meet,
Or thorns compose so rich a crown?

Were the whole realm of nature mine,
That were a present far too small:
Love so amazing, so divine,
Demands my soul, my life, my all.

Has your time spent at the cross produced this kind of response?

READ

Joseph took the body and wrapped it in a clean linen cloth.
—Matthew 27:59 NASB

In Jerusalem, lavish preparations are being made for the evening meal at Fortress Antonia. Pilate, exhausted from the long day's events, soberly sips a glass of wine. The Jew from Nazareth continues to plague his thoughts. Visions of death by crucifixion linger, and the procurator becomes increasingly agitated.

A persistent pounding at the door startles him from his morbid musing. A servant informs him that Joseph from the town of Arimathea, a member of the Sanhedrin, requests an audience. *Now what?* Pilate shakes his head. *Will this thing ever go away?* But Joseph is a wealthy and powerful man. It would not be prudent to refuse to see him. He instructs the servant to bring him in.

Joseph strides forward with brisk confidence. "Sir, it is the very sacred custom of my people to bury the dead before sundown. Time is short and I would like to request permission to take the body of Jesus of Nazareth and prepare it for burial."

Pilate examines the distinguished religious leader. How odd

that one of those responsible for Jesus' death would now want to give Him an honorable burial. Still, Pilate relishes the thought of being done with the whole thing.

"Is He dead, then?" he asks. "Let us find out."

A messenger is sent to question the centurion at Golgotha. He returns, assuring Pilate that Jesus has been dead now for some time. With great relief Pilate signs the orders to turn the corpse over to Joseph. At last, he can be rid of this perplexing stranger who turned his life upside down in one day.

Joseph hurries back to Golgotha, apprehension stirring within. What has compelled him to do such a thing? Surely he will lose everything—reputation, status, and perhaps even his livelihood. Why take such a risk? Does he regret not speaking up on Jesus' behalf just hours ago at the trial? Can it be that this is his first act of faith in the Messiah for whom he has so eagerly waited all his life? Or is he simply fulfilling his priestly duty to make sure that the dead are buried before sundown?

On the way out of town, Joseph stops at a market stall and purchases a large piece of clean, soft linen. As he approaches the incline up Golgotha, he is sickened by what he sees. Flies hover around the body of Christ and crows circle above, ready to devour the decaying flesh. He is shocked at Jesus' physical condition.

Sobered, he hands the orders to the centurion who reads the paper, glancing up at Joseph with relief and respect. He directs the other soldiers to the cross where Christ's emaciated body hangs. One of them grips the nail in Jesus' feet with a large tool, working it back and forth until it comes out. With the Y-shaped poles, they lift the crossbeam off the stipe and lay it on the ground.

Joseph watches, fighting emotions he can't explain as they remove the nails from Jesus' wrists. Pulling the beam from under the inert body, the centurion turns to him and nods. The honorable religious leader of the Jews kneels beside the form of a man he barely knew and surely never understood, grieved that he has waited so long to come to Him.

Laying the cloth out, he gently rolls the body onto it. The simple task distresses him. Scanning the horizon, he sees the soldiers already moving toward town. He must hurry—there is little time before sundown.

Joseph is not alone. A short distance away, a small group of women watch every move he makes. Though their hearts long to be the ones preparing their Rabbi for burial, they know they cannot approach this esteemed member of the Sanhedrin. They will watch and wait, for now.

Carefully he pulls the corners of the linen tightly together, then tucks them in. When the corpse is secure, he rises and calls for some servants to help carry it to the tomb he has prepared. The day of death is coming to an end.

Not long ago, this bruised and battered body was a beautiful baby, the Son of God full of life, wrapped in swaddling clothes, lying in a manger. There, a handful of shepherds and a choir of angels celebrated His birth.

Today, the lifeless corpse is wrapped in white linen, attended by a handful of heavy-hearted followers. But angel choirs surely wait in the wings now, songs of celebration on the tips of their tongues. For in the grand scheme of God's eternal plan, weeping may last for the night, but joy always comes in the morning.

RESPOND

There were probably many times Joseph of Arimathea could have spoken out on Christ's behalf. As a member of the Sanhedrin he attended both trials, watching them slap Jesus around and mock Him. It seems he never protested. John tells us that secretly he was a follower of Christ, yet feared the reaction of his peers. Spend some time looking at your own life. Are there times when you fail to speak the truth about Christ? When He is maligned do you keep quiet for fear of what others might think? Can you imagine the courage it must have taken for Joseph to reveal his commitment to Christ by asking for the body? In what areas of your walk with God do you long for this kind of courage?

Now, consider the women who have never left Jesus' side. See them standing afar, unable to intervene, to even wash the wounds of their beloved Teacher in death. Yet, they do not leave. What compels them to stay? What would compel you to commit yourself to Him with such fortitude?

Spend some time in prayer over these things. Read the following passage:

> *What I tell you in the darkness, speak in the light; and what you hear whispered in your ear, proclaim upon the housetops . . . Therefore everyone who confesses Me before men, I will also confess him before My Father who is in heaven. But whoever denies Me before men, I will also deny him before My Father who is in heaven.*
> —Matthew 10:27, 32–33 NASB

Meditate on these things. What is God saying to you? Write a prayer of response.

PRAYER

> *My Savior, my Friend—I can feel the sorrow in Joseph's heart as he wraps Your cold body. Oh, what he missed by waiting so long. And how much of You I have not yet understood, or known, or loved, because I wait when I could run to You. Banish the foolish fears and selfish passions that keep me from You—burn them like dross until my heart is pure, aflame with desire for You alone, oh living God.*

38   Myrrh and Aloe

> *In the cross is an ocean of love yet un-*
> *revealed, a mountain of power still un-*
> *released, and a sea of truth not yet fathomed*
> *. . . There is something utterly exhaustless*
> *about the provisions of Calvary.*
>
> —S. Franklin Logsdon

Reflect

Bring your heart before your heavenly Father today by slowly speaking the model prayer found below:

> *Our Father who is in heaven, hallowed be Your name.*
> *Your kingdom come. Your will be done, on earth as it is*
> *in heaven. Give us this day our daily bread. And forgive*
> *us our debts, as we also have forgiven our debtors. And*
> *do not lead us into temptation, but deliver us from evil.*
> *For Yours is the kingdom and the power and the glory*
> *forever. Amen.*
>
> —Matthew 6:9–13 NASB

Reflect on each phrase as you pray it, especially in light of what you have gleaned from contemplating the cross of Christ.

Read

> *All Your garments are fragrant with myrrh and aloes.*
> —Psalm 45:8 NASB

With the help of his servants, Joseph of Arimathea carries the corpse of Jesus of Nazareth down Golgotha. Travelers stop to stare. Why would a religious leader such as this become unclean by having anything to do with a dead body, especially that of a criminal?

Two women, Mary of Magdala and Mary the aunt of Jesus, continue to follow, bringing up the rear of the only funeral march Jesus will have. The masses who flocked to hear Him teach and watch Him perform miracles have disappeared. Those whose bodies were restored by His touch, or whose lonely hearts found compassion in His eyes, now busy themselves with Sabbath preparations.

Joseph turns at the bottom of the hill and walks several yards to the entrance of a lovely garden against the slope of Golgotha. The scent of spring blossoms fills the air, a pleasant respite from Calvary's rank residue. He directs the men to take the body through an opening carved in the rocky hillside. It is a fairly new sepulcher, no corpse having ever been laid there.

The two women approach, stationing themselves just outside the garden where they can see through the door into the rock-hewn tomb. They watch as Jesus' body is placed on a stone bench protruding from the wall of the cave. When the evening sky starts to grow dim, they know they must leave. Making plans to return with spices to anoint their Master after the Sabbath, they reluctantly head back toward town.

Joseph removes the linen cloth and begins tenderly washing the bruised body of Christ in preparation for burial. He finds the process therapeutic, a source of healing for his aching heart. As he finishes with the face, a commotion outside startles him. Peering out, he sees a fellow member of the Sanhedrin entering the garden followed by several servants bearing jars of rich-scented myrrh and aloes.

He steps outside and as their eyes meet, the two priests sense an unspoken camaraderie. Joseph understands all too well why Nicodemus comes now. He remembers rumors of him meeting with Jesus in the dark of night for religious discussion. He recalls the meeting of the council during the Feast of the Tabernacles when Caiaphas demanded Jesus' arrest. Nicodemus spoke boldly then, challenging the high priests to abide by their own laws and not condemn someone without hearing his defense.

Yet, like himself during the mockery of a trial before the Sanhedrin, Nicodemus said nothing in Jesus' favor. When he could have made a difference, he kept silent. But now, like Joseph, he can stay away no longer. Each man in his own way must struggle with his shame.

Joseph embraces his friend, kissing him on each cheek. Side by side, they carefully wash the mangled body, then begin the embalming process. They alternate wrapping the corpse with strips of cloth and sprinkling the powdered spices over it, leaving the head and face exposed. The aroma of aloes and myrrh allays the stench of decaying flesh. In this poignant sundown vigil, Joseph wraps and Nicodemus anoints the body of the Christ.

When they are finished, they carry the cadaver through a low opening into the dark recesses of the cave for final burial. Nicodemus takes a small cloth, saturates it with spices, and places it over Jesus' face. It is done.

Then they step out of the darkness into the cool evening air where Joseph locates a large boulder and calls for a group of servants to roll it across the entrance to the tomb. Hearts full of grief and regret, the two priests embrace in farewell, hurrying to perform sacred duties and join their families for Sabbath.

The Son of Man, who never had a place to lay His head, is now put to rest in a rich man's grave. The Lamb whose sacrifice on Calvary drifted like a pleasing aroma to the Father is now anointed with sweet-smelling spices fit for a king. As families light the evening candles and pray, the body that once held the Light of the World rots in a cold, dark cave. It seems the final act of humankind's greatest tragedy has come to an end.

RESPOND

Consider the heart of Nicodemus. He was a true seeker who asked sincere questions of Christ when he came to Him at night. How hard it was for him to let go of his religious preconceptions in order to trust the truth of Christ's words. Do you cling to anything today that keeps you from hearing Jesus' voice to you? Religious works? Spiritual busyness? Christian reputation? Ask God to show you what you must leave behind as you come to Jesus in His death.

In the fourth century, a church leader named Augustine wrote the following words about his own conversion. Read them slowly, savoring their depth.

> *Belatedly I loved thee, O Beauty so ancient and so new, belatedly I loved thee. For see, thou wast within and I was without, and I sought thee out there . . . Thou didst call and cry aloud, and didst force open my deafness. Thou didst gleam and shine, and didst chase away my blindness. Thou didst breathe fragrant odors and I drew in my breath; and now I pant for thee. I tasted, and now I hunger and thirst. Thou didst touch me, and I burned for thy peace.*
>
> —Saint Augustine's *Confessions*, Book 10

Write a prayer to Jesus, anointing Him with the aromatic spices of your own words.

PRAYER

> *Lord, they rolled the stone and sealed Your body in darkness. It is so hard for me to grasp that it was only a shell—that You were no part of those burial preparations. I see how often I run after things I hope will bring You pleasure, but I am too late, for I've been consumed with dead deeds and lifeless works. I want to learn to hear You*

in the echoes of silence, dear Lord—to see the flickering flame of love through the darkness of Your seeming distance. I don't want to miss You, sweet Savior of mine— hold my head to Your heart and let me hear only the sound of it beating in my ear.

39   The Sabbath

Nowhere do I more find such fruitful still-
ness as when I am near the cross. Nowhere
do I feel so inclined to take the shoes from
off my feet. And how do you account for it?
— John Henry Jowett

Reflect

Make this time with God a time of rest as the Jews did on the Sabbath. Mentally cease from all activity except focusing on Him. Breathe deeply and slowly. Feel the coolness of the earth in the dark tomb where Christ has been laid. Smell the aromatic spices. Anticipate the miraculous as you offer yourself to the Savior. Ask Him to reveal His truth to your own heart today.

Read the following verses aloud as a proclamation of praise and preparation in your own heart for what God will do:

> *Lift up your heads, O gates, and be lifted up, O ancient*
> *doors, that the King of glory may come in! Who is the*
> *King of glory? The LORD strong and mighty, the LORD*
> *mighty in battle. Lift up your heads, O gates, and lift*
> *them up, O ancient doors, that the King of glory may*
> *come in! Who is this King of glory? The LORD of hosts,*
> *He is the King of glory. Selah.*
> — Psalm 24:7–10 NASB

Write a prayer to Jesus, opening the way for Him to enter the gates of the various parts of your life.

READ

There remains a Sabbath rest for the people of God.
—Hebrews 4:9 NASB

The setting sun ushers in a High Holy Day for the Jews in Jerusalem as they celebrate both Sabbath and the Feast of Unleavened Bread. Fathers in homes throughout the city regale their children with tales of their ancestors' miraculous exodus from Egypt long ago.

The forced rest provides much time for reflection and quietness. Even the simplest tasks are left undone, and all of the market stalls owned by Jews have closed until the sun sets tomorrow afternoon. In obedience, both pilgrims who have come to Jerusalem for Passover and those who live here join together to keep the Sabbath Day holy.

Not everyone rests, however. A small group of women huddle together in one home, consumed with sadness at the events they have witnessed over the past several hours. Every now and then someone asks Mary of Magdala to describe once again what she saw at the tomb owned by the priest named Joseph. Through the long night, no one even thinks of trying to sleep.

The men who once followed Christ mourn His death in a room upstairs. It is a sorrowful Sabbath indeed for these whose hope resided in Jesus the Teacher. How they grieve. What must they feel? Hopelessness? Disillusionment? Fear? Anger? Does the thought of a future without their beloved Master riddle them with anxiety? Do they second-guess the trust they once had, feeling foolish at their gullibility? Or are they simply numb with shock?

Several members of the Sanhedrin are spending the night hours gathered in the temple, discussing concerns about the crucified Carpenter. Fearing that Jesus will become more of a hero in death than He was in life, Caiaphas decides to go to Pilate and demand action.

The procurator, already weighed down with weariness, is

put off when the priests arrive. Hasn't he done everything these zealots want? Why are they bothering him now? Again and again last night he awoke sweating from a nightmare in which his hands were covered with blood and his wife was screaming at him.

He enters the courtyard, beckoning for Caiaphas to approach. "What is it?"

"Sir, we have been talking and we remember that the deceiver Jesus, when He was still alive, said He would rise again after three days. Of course we don't believe this foolishness, but we are concerned that His disciples might come and steal the body. Then they would tell all our people that He did rise, and things will be worse than when He was alive."

Pilate watches the influential religious leader. He can hardly stand the man with his oily tongue and false humility. But suddenly he is tired of dealing with him. "You may have your guard—go with them and make the grave as secure as you can."

The priests accompany the contingent of Roman soldiers to Joseph's tomb where a stone is already in place. They pull it back, and one ducks inside to make sure the body is still there. After securing the tomb to their satisfaction, the priests leave the guards in place, returning to the temple for Sabbath sacrifices.

Within the dark bowels of a grave, the empty frame of Jesus rests. But all is not as it seems. While disheartened followers grieve and Pharisees breathe sighs of relief, the Spirit of Christ moves throughout the cosmos, crashing through Hades' gates to proclaim victory over sin and death. In the pit of hell, fallen angels rage at the Son of God, who lives after all.

There has never been another Sabbath Day like this one. Mary and the others, as women are wont to do, channel their pain into plans for embalming the body of Christ. Religious leaders conduct Passover rituals, and distraught disciples disappear from sight. But all the while, the Lord of the Sabbath prepares for the event that will soon send shock waves around the world and change forever the course of history.

RESPOND

Spend some time imagining the thoughts and feelings of Jesus' followers on this day. Apparently, they had no remembrance or understanding of Jesus' promises concerning His resurrection. All they knew was what they saw in front of them. Can you imagine the despair? The darkness? The lonely ache in their guts? Try to imagine what it would be like during this time, to not have a clue that something wonderful was about to break into your horror.

Thank God for the reality of His presence through His Spirit in your life. Experience His commitment to live within you, and work through you. Enjoy the truth that He has chosen you, that He longs for you and loves to commune with you. Rest for a time with these thoughts.

PRAYER

Mighty Jesus—whirling in Spirit throughout the universe, proclaiming victory while Your followers mourn. I see myself in them, Lord—embracing the dance of death, while You declare life. I long to live in the realm where You move and work, though hope seems sealed up in tombs. Teach me, Almighty God, the assurance of things not seen, the confidence of things hoped for—the secret of resurrection faith.

THE RESURRECTION

The disciples had seen the strong hands of
God twist the crown of thorns into a crown
of glory, and in hands as strong as that they
knew themselves safe . . . They had
expected a walkover, and they beheld a vic-
tory; they had expected an earthly Messiah,
and they beheld the Soul of Eternity.

—Dorothy L. Sayers

REFLECT

Today is a day of victory and celebration—a confirmation of
the hope that we have in our hearts through the Holy Spirit
who lives there. Begin with a time of thanksgiving for all God
has done for you, especially in view of the Cross.

Read or sing the words to the following hymn, offering a
heart of deep joy and awe-filled worship:

Crown Him with Many Crowns
Matthew Bridges/George J. Elvey

Crown Him with many crowns,
The Lamb upon His throne;
Hark! how the heavenly anthem drowns
All music but its own.
Awake, my soul, and sing
Of Him who died for thee,
And hail Him as thy matchless King
Through all eternity.

Crown Him the Lord of life,
Who triumphed o'er the grave,
And rose victorious in the strife
For those He came to save;
His glories now we sing
Who died and rose on high,
Who died, eternal life to bring,
And lives, that death may die.

Crown Him the Lord of love;
Behold His hands and side,
Those wounds, yet visible above,
In beauty glorified.
All hail, Redeemer, hail!
For Thou hast died for me;
Thy praise and glory shall not fail
Throughout eternity.

READ

I have seen the Lord.
—John 20:18 NASB

When the last of Saturday's sun begins to sink below the horizon, the long Sabbath ends, propelling the women into action. Three go to purchase more supplies while the marketplace is still open. Upon their return, tender hands crush and mix dried flowers and pungent spices for hours, all of them soberly sharing this final act of compassion as another night without their beloved Jesus passes by.

When morning nears, they hurry off to the tomb. After walking some distance, one of the women wonders aloud if a stone will seal the entrance into the cave. What will they do if it does? Surely they won't have the strength to move it. A discussion ensues concerning whether they should get one of the men. But they are almost there, and no one wants to turn back now.

In the predawn darkness, soldiers stand and stretch, tired from the long night. As the morning watch moves into position, the ground begins to shake under their feet. Astonished, the guards cannot believe their eyes when a dazzling creature descends as if from nowhere. With a face like lightning and clothed in brilliant white, the angel rolls the stone away and takes a seat at the top.

Every single guard faints at the sight. Coming to only seconds later, they stumble over one another as they rush frantically into the cave. Panic ensues as they scan its crevices and see for themselves that there is no body there. Gripped by fear, the entire group races back toward Jerusalem, dreading Pilate's response to what has just happened.

The sun creeps slowly across the eastern sky, though the tomb is still shrouded in darkness as the women arrive. Relieved that there is no stone blocking the sepulcher's entrance, two of them go inside, only to be devastated at what they find. The body of Jesus is not there.

As they stand forlorn and confused, the cave is suddenly bathed in light revealing the presence of two men in shining robes. Falling in fear to the ground, the women hear a message that seems beyond belief: "Why are you looking in a tomb for Someone who is alive? He is not here—He is risen! Don't you remember what He said—that the Messiah must be betrayed by evil men and be crucified, and that He would rise again on the third day?"

The two women glance at each other, then tear from the cave. Followed by the others, they run back to Jerusalem where the disciples continue to mourn. Breathless, they tell the men what they have just seen.

The disciples stare at them as if they are crazy, dismissing their words as superstitious nonsense. Blinded by grief, each man returns to his unique brand of sorrow.

Mary Magdalene, distraught by their response, pleads with Peter and John to believe her. "They have taken the Lord's body—it is gone and I don't know where they have placed it."

Something in her voice stirs them. The two men hurry from the house through the streets of the city to the tomb of Joseph of Arimathea. John, being younger and faster, arrives first. He bends down and sees the empty cloths, but stays back, afraid. Peter catches up quickly and crashes into the cave, determined to discover the truth.

There on the stone bench lie the linen cloths completely undisturbed, as if a body just disappeared within the folds. On the side lies the headpiece in a tidy roll. Slowly, faith begins to fill the crevices of Peter's broken heart.

John joins him in the cave and together they share a moment of pure incredulity. Words from the past echo through their minds. The Rabbi had told them He would rise again—could it be? Is it possible? Can they dare hope? Thoughtfully they walk in silence back to town.

Mary Magdalene, having followed them to the tomb, watches them leave. She begins to weep, stooping down one more time to peer into the empty grave. But this time it isn't empty. On either end of the bench where she'd seen them lay Christ, are two white-robed angels.

"Why do you cry?" one asks.

"Because they've taken my Lord away, and I don't know where they put Him."

Sobbing by now, Mary hears a sound behind her. She looks over her shoulder, and the sight of a gardener gives her a glimmer of hope. "Sir, please—if you have taken Him away, just tell me where, and I will go and get Him."

"Mary."

She freezes. Only one person has ever spoken her name like that. Long ago, when tortured by demons and having no hope of ever finding peace, she met Jesus of Nazareth. How can she ever forget the moment when He called out, "Mary," and light rushed in, expelling the dark forces that had almost destroyed her? The scene flashes through her mind as she turns to face the One who speaks.

"Master!" Mary exclaims, rushing toward Him.

"Wait, Mary—you cannot cling to Me now, for I haven't yet ascended to My Father. You must go and find My brothers. Tell them that I ascend to My Father and your Father, My God and your God."

Then He is gone. Mary stands for a moment in complete amazement at what she has seen and heard. Tears stream down her cheeks as she turns to run back to the disciples. "I have seen the Lord," she tells them. The look in her eyes and wonder in her voice leave no room for doubt that, indeed, she has encountered the risen Christ.

I have seen the Lord. Resurrection hope is spawned in that moment, then spreads like a soothing ointment to all who will believe—some having seen, and others simply by faith—that what Jesus of Nazareth said He would do, He did. And resurrection hope transcends time, instilling eternity in the hearts of humankind.

RESPOND

Can you even comprehend what Mary must have felt when she heard the voice of Jesus saying her name as only He could say it? Stop and sense the wonder, the joy, and the hope that must have encompassed her complete being. Place yourself there in the time, bringing with you all your fears, your unfulfilled dreams and disappointments. Hear Jesus speaking your name. Listen. Hear it again.

Fall at His feet and worship Him. Say aloud, "I have seen the Lord." Now see yourself running to those you know and those you don't know. Speak it in the streets and shout it from the mountaintops: "I have seen the Lord." Run to a world lost and dying in darkness and share with them the hope of a risen Savior.

Celebrate! Rejoice! Sing! Shout! Jump for joy! Dance with all your might! The Lord lives! He is worthy! Give thanks! Give Him the honor and praise due His holy name! HE IS RISEN! ALLELUIA! For the Lord our God the Omnipotent reigns!

PRAYER

Oh, my Master, simple joy so fills my heart that I have no words to speak. You are not dead. You are alive. You have defeated death. And I, too, will live with You for eternity. How I long for the day when I will see You face-to-face, dearest Redeemer. I will kiss Your nail-scarred feet again and again, and I will touch Your wounded side, holding Your battered hands to my face. There I will stay, proclaiming forever, "I have seen the Lord."

EPILOGUE

The Rest of the Story

Paul Harvey, well-known American radio commentator, is famous for revealing surprise endings to unusual stories and little-known facts about popular news items. He ends every broadcast with the now-famous line: "And that, my friends, is the rest of the story." What might Mr. Harvey say about the nondescript Jew from Nazareth who died on a cross more than two thousand years ago? Perhaps it would go something like this:

On the third day after his death, Jesus of Nazareth miraculously arose, culminating the fulfillment of more than three hundred prophecies from the Hebrew Scriptures. He appeared at least ten times to those who knew Him, and to as many as five hundred people at one time. This was no short-lived hallucination on the part of fanatic followers. He ate with them, exhorted and encouraged them, and let doubters touch the holes in His body from the spear and nails. After forty days He ascended into the clouds in plain view of all, accompanied by angels who promised He would come again one day just as He had left.

What of the other participants in the drama of Christ's death? The high priest Annas continued a tradition of greed and repression. He raised money by extortion and bribed Roman procurators, all while claiming to represent God. Early records reveal his tomb near the south wall of Jerusalem.

Annas's son-in-law, Caiaphas, enjoyed the longest reign of any chief priest in the first century. He remained a shrewd strategist and politician, enabling his lengthy regime. His family tomb was recently discovered on the south wall of Jerusalem.

Herod Antipas, the Jewish tetrarch, cultivated his friendship with the Roman emperor Tiberius, even building a town in his honor. All the while he sought to expand his own authority, secretly craving the kind of rule his father, Herod the Great, had known. In AD 39 he was found guilty of treason and banished to Lyones, stripped of all wealth and power. He and his wife, Herodias, died later in Spain.

In Pilate's ten-year reign, he had numerous conflicts with the Jews. One time he overstepped his bounds, having hundreds of Samaritan Jews executed by Roman soldiers. Ordered to return to Rome, he never arrived. Tradition states that while on the way there, he committed suicide, not willing to face a Roman trial. Coins depicting pagan sacrifices and bearing his name that were produced while he ruled in Jerusalem are some of the only physical evidence of Pilate's existence.

The accusers and mockers of Jesus Christ are gone, little more than a footnote in history. In fact, none of them would be worthy of mention were it not for their role in His death.

Yet those who followed Christ made an amazing comeback after He arose. The small band of men who were too afraid to attend the Crucifixion were transformed at Pentecost when Jesus poured out His Holy Spirit upon them. In the coming years they would turn the world upside down with their fervor to spread the truth about their Master, all but one being martyred for their faith.

In every generation since, believers have boldly and joyfully taken the message of the Cross to others—an unstoppable force—even at great personal risk. Though seventy million people have died for daring to declare the good news of Jesus Christ since AD 33, Christianity now spans the globe as the world's largest religion, encompassing almost one-third of its population.

There is no doubt that Jesus Christ altered the course of history. Even a casual glance at a calendar affirms the reality of His existence two thousand years ago. No one has ever changed individual lives as Jesus of Nazareth has. No one has ever affected the world order as He has. Jesus is not only the most unique person of all time, but through the power of His resurrection, continues to put hope in the hearts of those looking for life's true meaning.

Perhaps one of the most apt descriptions of this Man is found every year on Christmas cards all over the world. The author is anonymous, but the words powerful:

Nineteen wide centuries have come and gone, and today He is the centerpiece of the human race and the leader of the column of progress. I am far within the mark when I say that all the armies that ever marched and all the navies that ever were built, and all of the parliaments that ever have sat, and all the kings that ever reigned put together have not affected the life of man upon this earth as powerfully as has that one solitary life, Jesus of Nazareth.

And that, my friends, is the rest of the story.

SUGGESTIONS FOR SMALL GROUP CONTEMPLATION

FORMAT: Each week will follow the same basic format but can be altered to meet the specific needs of the group. It will use a unique method of group study/contemplation based on a rich tradition called *lectio divina*, which has been practiced throughout biblical history.[1]

FACILITATOR: A facilitator will be needed to help the group move through the times of prayer, reading, and contemplation. This may be one person or several group members who alternate weeks. The facilitator should acquaint him- or herself thoroughly with the meeting format ahead of time. Each week, the facilitator will choose one person or several to take turns reading the suggested passage. If the group is large, it may be helpful to divide into smaller units after the initial prayer focus each week.

ASSIGNMENTS: Though this study can be done anytime during the year, for group purposes the daily devotionals are assigned to match a normal Lenten schedule—four the first week (beginning on Ash Wednesday) and six each week following until Easter, with Sundays off.

---

1. The format suggested has been taken from the ancient Benedictine practice of *Lectio Divina*. For a more thorough treatment, see *Accepting the Embrace of God: The Ancient Art of Lectio Divina*, by Fr. Luke Dysinger, O.S.B. http://www.valyermo.com/ld-art.html.

WEEKLY MEETING FORMAT

INITIAL PRAYER FOCUS: Each meeting will begin with a specific prayer focus provided for you. You may have one person pray aloud on behalf of the group, have group members take turns praying aloud, or ask all to participate in a time of silent prayer.

SCRIPTURE READING AND CONTEMPLATION

FIRST READING: The purpose of this reading is for each member to hear the Holy Spirit speak some specific word or phrase from the passage about who God is, what His character is like, how He works, etc.

— One person reads the passage aloud slowly and meditatively **two times**.
— The group waits in silence for one to two minutes, listening, pondering the word or phrase that has captured their attention.
— Each member of the group shares the word or phrase that spoke to them in a simple statement (not teaching or expounding).

SECOND READING: The purpose of this reading is for the listeners to ask the Holy Spirit to speak to them about how God relates to them and the world.

— Have a different person read the same passage aloud, slowly.
— The group waits in silence again for two to three minutes, asking God the question: "What is the critical message You are speaking?" and waiting for the answer.
— Each member of the group shares what they have heard God speaking by making brief statements like "I hear . . ." or "I see . . ."

THIRD READING: The purpose of this reading is for the group members to discover what action God would have them take in response to what they have heard from Him today.

— Have a third person read the passage aloud, slowly.
— In silence, each person reflects on the question: "God, what do You want me to do, see, be . . . today?"
— Each person shares what he or she has heard and gained from their reflection on the passage, and what they would like prayer for. This can be a little longer than the previous sharing.

ENDING PRAYER: During this time you will pray for one another, based on what has just been shared. You may divide into pairs or, if your group is small, have each person pray aloud for the person on their right. Another method is to have a time of silence, asking each person to pray for the people on either side of him or her, ending with oral prayer by the facilitator.

WEEK ONE

This meeting should take place before the forty-day journey begins. (If done as a Lenten devotional, this meeting needs to take place before Ash Wednesday.) During this time you will make sure group members have books, answer questions, and establish your meeting place and time. The facilitator will need to be prepared to read through the instructions for the meeting format with the group, explaining the weekly process of *lectio divina*. Once business is taken care of and the group understands the format, begin as follows:

INITIAL PRAYER FOCUS: Open by having group members offer up words of praise and thanksgiving to God. After a season of praise, ask group members to divide into groups of two or three and share what they hope to gain from this journey to the cross. When they are finished, have them pray for this season of focusing on the Cross together. (This should take no more than ten minutes.)

SCRIPTURE READING AND CONTEMPLATION (*Lectio Divina*): John 16:1–16. If you haven't already done so, assign the three reading times to different people. (See the initial meeting format.)

ENDING PRAYER: Choose a method of praying for one another as noted in the initial meeting format.

FINAL NOTE: Encourage group members to journal their prayers as they are guided in the forty-day cross journey. Ask them to bring these to your group meetings, as you will have them share them in prayer from time to time.

ASSIGNMENT FOR WEEK ONE: Days 1–4

WEEK TWO

By now members will have begun doing the daily devotionals. Start by having volunteers share what the first leg of this journey has meant to them, what has surprised them, or what has troubled them about what they have seen.

INITIAL PRAYER FOCUS: Make this prayer time focus exclusively on thanksgiving. Here are some ideas:

1. Go around the circle, asking each person to give thanks aloud for three things.
2. Have a season of prayer in which group members take turns giving thanks aloud in short and spontaneous prayers.
3. Have one person lead aloud while the others give thanks silently.

SCRIPTURE READING AND CONTEMPLATION (*Lectio Divina*): John 16:17–24. If it hasn't been done, assign the three reading times to different people. (Follow the initial meeting format.)

ENDING PRAYER: End the time together by first praying for one another, then asking each participant to read aloud one of their written prayers from the past days of their cross journey, or to pray a short spontaneous prayer.

ASSIGNMENT FOR WEEK TWO: Days 5–10

WEEK THREE

Now that the group members are several days into the journey, ask each one to share the highlight of their time so far.

INITIAL PRAYER FOCUS: Structure this prayer time as one of

praise for the different names of God. (Scripture provides hundreds of names like Jehovah, Adonai, Lion of Judah, Bread of Life, etc.) Ask the group members to simply offer up the names that come to mind in praise. (For example, *I praise You, Living Water, for You have given me to drink over and over,* or *I thank You, Lion of Judah, for You always wage war on my behalf.*) Two passages of Scripture members can look to for help are Isaiah 9:6 or Revelation 1:5–8.

SCRIPTURE READING AND CONTEMPLATION (*Lectio Divina*): John 16:25–33. If it hasn't been done, assign the three reading times to different people. (Follow the initial meeting format.)

ENDING PRAYER: End the time together by first praying for one another, and then asking each participant to read aloud one of their written prayers from the past days of their cross journey, or to pray a short spontaneous prayer.

ASSIGNMENT FOR WEEK THREE: Days 11–16

WEEK FOUR

Begin with a time of sharing concerning how this journey to the cross is impacting the participant's relationship with Christ. Ask probing questions such as: *Has this journey caused you to see Jesus in a different way? How? In what ways are you seeing and handling sin differently as a result of what you've seen? How would you say you see God's love now, as compared to before you began this journey?*

INITIAL PRAYER FOCUS: Divide the group into two groups and alternate reading the following aloud from Psalm 67 as the opening prayer time. Ask one person to lead in prayer to close this prayer time.

Group One: God be gracious to us and bless us, and cause His face to shine upon us— Selah.

Group Two: That Your way may be known on the earth, Your salvation among all nations.

Group One: Let the peoples praise You, O God; let all the peoples praise You.

Group Two: Let the nations be glad and sing for joy;

Group One: For You will judge the peoples with uprightness and guide the nations on the earth. Selah.

Group Two: Let the peoples praise You, O God; let all the peoples praise You.

Group One: The earth has yielded its produce; God, our God, blesses us.

Group Two: God blesses us, that all the ends of the earth may fear Him. (NASB)

SCRIPTURE READING AND CONTEMPLATION (*Lectio Divina*): John 17:1–5. If it hasn't been done, assign the three reading times to different people. (Follow the initial meeting format.)

ENDING PRAYER: End the time together by first praying for one another, then asking each participant to read aloud one of their written prayers from the past days of their cross journey, or to pray a short spontaneous prayer.

ASSIGNMENT FOR WEEK FOUR: Days 17–22

WEEK FIVE

Spend some time discussing the wounds of Christ that have been seen so far. Some would say that Christ endured every kind of human suffering we might encounter in our lives in the hours of His Passion. Do participants agree? What are some examples, beginning with the Garden of Gethsemane?

INITIAL PRAYER FOCUS: Let this prayer time be a focus on the attributes of God. Have participants turn to Psalm 145 and offer prayers aloud based on any attributes they see there.

SCRIPTURE READING AND CONTEMPLATION (*Lectio Divina*): John 17:6–19. If it hasn't been done, assign the three reading times to different people. (Follow the initial meeting format.)

ENDING PRAYER: End the time together by first praying for one another first, then asking each participant to read aloud one of their written prayers from the past days of their cross journey, or to pray a short spontaneous prayer.

ASSIGNMENT FOR WEEK FIVE: Days 23–28

WEEK SIX

Open the time with a discussion about the feelings of the various Passion participants such as John, Mary, a centurion, Caiaphas, God the Father, or Satan (choose one or as many as time allows). What were they experiencing? How was this impacting them? What did they really understand at this point? How do participants relate to them?

INITIAL PRAYER FOCUS: Ask each group member to offer a prayer of thanksgiving for what they have seen of Jesus in His suffering that truly blesses them. Go around the group so that each person can do this aloud. If someone prefers to not pray aloud, ask them to simply say "Pass" and continue to pray silently.

SCRIPTURE READING AND CONTEMPLATION (*Lectio Divina*): John 17:20–26. If it hasn't been done, assign the three reading times to different people. (Follow the initial meeting format.)

ENDING PRAYER: End the time together by first praying for one another, then asking each participant to read aloud one of their written prayers from the past days of their cross journey, or to pray a short spontaneous prayer.

ASSIGNMENT FOR WEEK SIX: Days 29–34

WEEK SEVEN

This may be the final group meeting (see note on Week Eight). Plan to bring some closure by looking toward the future and God's purposes for participants. Begin by asking the group members to share how they think this journey has changed the way they will approach daily living—relationships to family or friends, career, church, etc.

INITIAL PRAYER FOCUS: The psalm Jesus very likely sang with His disciples at the Last Supper was Psalm 118 (a common Passover hymn). Divide the group into two parts, and read the following excerpts from this psalm as the opening prayer, pondering how Jesus and His disciples might have felt as they sang it.

Group One: Give thanks to the LORD, for he is good; his love endures forever. Let Israel say: "His love endures forever." Let the house of Aaron say: "His love endures forever." Let those who fear the LORD say: "His love endures forever."

Group Two: In my anguish I cried to the LORD, and he answered by setting me free. The LORD is with me; I will not be afraid. What can man do to me? The LORD is with me; he is my helper. I will look in triumph on my enemies.

Group One: It is better to take refuge in the LORD than to trust in man. It is better to take refuge in the LORD than to trust in princes . . . The LORD is my strength and my song; he has become my salvation.

Group Two: Shouts of joy and victory resound in the tents of the righteous: "The LORD's right hand has done mighty things! The LORD's right hand is lifted high; the LORD's right hand has done mighty things!" I will not die but live, and will proclaim what the LORD has done . . .

Group One: Open for me the gates of righteousness; I will enter and give thanks to the LORD. This is the gate of the LORD through which the righteous may enter. I will give you thanks, for you answered me; you have become my salvation.

Group Two: The stone the builders rejected has become the capstone; the LORD has done this, and it is marvelous in our eyes. This is the day the LORD has made; let us rejoice and be glad in it . . .

Group One: The LORD is God, and he has made his light shine upon us. With boughs in hand, join in the festal procession up to the horns of the altar. You are my God, and I will give you thanks; you are my God, and I will exalt you.

All: Give thanks to the LORD, for he is good; his love endures forever. (vv. 1–9, 14–17, 19–24, 27–29 NIV)

SCRIPTURE READING AND CONTEMPLATION (*Lectio Divina*): Acts 1:1–10. If it hasn't been done, assign the three reading times to different people. (Follow the initial meeting format.)

ENDING PRAYER: End the time together by first praying for one another, then asking each participant to read aloud one of their written prayers from the past days of their cross journey, or to pray a short spontaneous prayer. End by saying the Lord's Prayer (Our Father) together.

ASSIGNMENT FOR WEEK SEVEN: Days 35–40

CELEBRATION: WEEK EIGHT (OPTIONAL)

If the group wants to meet once more at the conclusion of the study, plan for it to be a time of sharing and celebration (perhaps plan to enjoy a celebration meal together). Instead of the normal format, have group members share, using any of the following questions for discussion:

1. What is one thing you learned about the Cross that you think will have a continuing impact on you?
2. What are some things you learned about the character of God that perhaps you hadn't really seen before?
3. Why do you think it is important to regularly focus on the sufferings of Christ?
4. Which day do you recall as having the single most impact on you? Why?
5. How might your view of the Resurrection differ after having contemplated the Cross?

End the time with extended praise and thanksgiving. If possible, spend some time singing and offering worship to the exalted Christ.

Resources

Adels, Jill Haak. *The Wisdom of the Saints*. New York: Oxford University Press, 1987.

Barbet, Pierre. *A Physician at Calvary*. Translated by the Earl of Wicklow. New York: PJ Kenedy & Sons, 1953.

Bishop, Jim. *The Day Christ Died*. San Francisco: HarperSanFrancisco, 1957.

Brown, Raymond E. *The Death of the Messiah: From Gethsemane to the Grave*, vols. I and II. New York: Doubleday, 1994.

Cantalamessa, Raniero. *Life in the Lordship of Christ*. Kansas City, MO: Sheed & Ward, 1990.

Card, Michael. *Immanuel: Reflections on the Life of Christ*. Nashville: Thomas Nelson, 1990.

Chambers, J. Oswald. *The Philosophy of Sin*. Fort Washington, PA: Christian Literature Crusade, 1960.

——. *My Utmost for His Highest*. New York: Dodd, Mead, & Company, 1935.

——. *The Place of Help*. Fort Washington, PA: Christian Literature Crusade, 1935.

Davis, C. Truman. "A Physician Testifies About the Crucifixion." The Review of the NEWS, April 14, 1976.

Edersheim, Alfred. *Jesus the Messiah*. New York: Longmans, Green & Co., 1898.

Edwards, Wm D., Wesley J. Gabel, and Floyd Hosmer. "On the Physical Death of Jesus Christ." In *Journal of the American Medical Association*, March 21, 1986, vol. 256.

Fosbroke, Hughell. *By Means of Death*. Greenwich, CT: Seabury Press, 1956.

Hession, Roy. *We Would See Jesus*. Fort Washington, PA: Christian Literature Crusade, 1958.

Kiehl, Erich H. *The Passion of Our Lord*. Grand Rapids: Baker Book House, 1990.

Logsdon, S. Franklin. *Lingering at Calvary*. Chicago: Moody Bible Institute, 1956.

Manning, Brennan. *The Signature of Jesus on the Pages of Our Lives*. Sisters, OR: Multnomah, 1992.

March, R. E. *The Greatest Theme in the World*. New York: Gospel Publishing House, 1908.

McGrath, Alister E. *The Mystery of the Cross*. Grand Rapids: Zondervan, 1988.

Morris, Leon. *The Cross of Jesus*. Grand Rapids: Wm. B. Eerdman's, 1988.

———. *The Atonement: Its Meaning and Significance*. England: Intervarsity Press, 1983.

———. *The Apostolic Preaching of the Cross*. London: Tyndale Press, 1955.

Motter, Alton M. *Preaching the Passion*. Philadelphia: Fortress, 1963.

Murphy, Richard, T.A. *Days of Glory: The Passion, Death, and*

Murray, Andrew. *The Blood of the Cross*. New Jersey: Fleming Revelle, n.d.

———. *The Cross of Christ*. Grand Rapids: Zondervan, 1989.

Resurrection of Jesus Christ. Ann Arbor, MI: Servant Books, 1980.

Robertson, A. T. *A Harmony of the Gospels*. New York: Harper & Row, 1950.

Slaughter, Frank G. *The Crown and the Cross*. New York: World, 1960.

Stott, John R. *The Cross of Christ*. Downers Grove, IL: InterVarsity Press, 1986.

Wangerin, Walter, Jr. *The Book of God: The Bible as a Novel*. Grand Rapids: Zondervan, 1996.

———. *Reliving the Passion*. Grand Rapids: Zondervan, 1992.

Whyte, Alexander. *The Best of Alexander Whyte*. Grand Rapids: Baker Book House, 1953.

Wiersbe, Warren, editor. *Classic Sermons on the Cross of Christ*. Grand Rapids: Kregel, 1990.

ABOUT THE AUTHOR

Tricia McCary Rhodes is the author of four books on the subject of prayer and the cross. With a B.A. in Psychology and an M.S. in Applied Social Resarch, Tricia spent two years as a missionary in the Alaska bush and currently travels to minister in remote areas of countries such as India and Bangladesh. In 1981 she and her husband, Joe, started New Hope Church in San Diego. She is a regular contributor to *Pray!* magazine and *Discipleship Journal* and has written articles for *Guideposts*, *Decision*, and *Moody Monthly*. The mother of two sons and grandmother of one, Tricia believes God's call on her life is to help others deepen their intimacy with Christ through prayer.

To learn more about Tricia Rhodes and her ministry, see www.soulatrest.com.